Intercultural Education in European Classrooms

Intercultural Education Partnership

Intercultural Education in European Classrooms

Intercultural Education Partnership

Edited by Susan Shaw

Trentham Books

Stoke on Trent, UK and Sterling, USA

Trentham Books Limited

Westview House	22883 Quicksilver Drive
734 London Road	Sterling
Oakhill	VA 20166-2012
Stoke on Trent	USA
Staffordshire	
England ST4 5NP	

First published 2000

British Library Cataloguing-in-Publication Data
A catalogue record for this book is available from the British Library

1 85856 169 8 (paperback)

Designed and typeset by Trentham Print Design Ltd., Chester and printed in Great Britain by Cromwell Press Ltd., Wiltshire.

This publication has been made possible through financial assistance from the Community of European Union which supported the networking, liaison, collaboration and research of partners working in the field of Intercultural Education across Europe.

The following pages are a result of the work of some partner-members of the Intercultural Education Partnership UK. Many of the chapters have been presented at symposia or conferences of partner members. The opinions and findings are those of the authors and do not necessarily represent the views of the Intercultural Education Partnership UK.

Contents

Notes on Authors

Carrie Cable is a lecturer in the School of Education at the Open University. She has taught in primary and secondary schools and been head of a Section 11 project in a London LEA. Her research interests include language development and continuing professional development in the field of EAL.

Dr Jim Cummins teaches courses related to language learning and critical pedagogy at the Ontario Institute for Studies in Education at the University of Toronto and has written widely on second language learning. His recent book *Negotiating Identities – Education for Empowerment in a Diverse Society* (California Association for Bilingual Education, 1996) reveals how relationships between educators and students are at the heart of learning and that these interactions always require a negotiation of identities. He is co-author of an ESL program *ScottForesman ESL: Accelerating English Language Learning* (ScottForesman, 1996).

Dr Viv Edwards is Professor of Language and Education and Director of the Reading and Language Information Centre at the University of Reading in the UK. She has written many books about the theory, pedagogy and practice of teaching and learning reading for bilingual learners in UK schools and particularly works to support classroom based research by teachers, as exemplified by *The Power of Babel* (Trentham Books, 1998).

Anna Hirvonen is Deputy Headteacher at Myllypuro Comprehensive School in Helsinki in Finland and has a particular interest in research into dual language learning.

Susan Jaine is a freelance education consultant in English as an Additional Language and Language in Education. Based in London, she provides advice and training on EAL and language related issues in schools and training environments in the region. She also writes conference reports and articles on her specialisms.

Joke Kypriotakis is Headteacher of Beatrixschool, Rotterdam in The Netherlands. She was on the editorial board for 'Sharing Practice in Intercultural Education' – a series of five publications arising from a trans-European project supported by The Socrates Programme of the Commission of the European Union – published by the Intercultural Education Partnership.

Dr Constant Leung is senior lecturer in the School of Education, King's College, London. He has taught in schools and universities in Hong Kong and England. His research interests include second language pedagogy in the mainstream curriculum, second language assessment and language policy. Professionally, he has been active in the promotion of in-service teacher education and was the founding chair of the National Association for Language Development in the Curriculum (NALDIC). He has published widely in the fields of applied linguistics and second language education.

Kostas Magos works as a teacher and teacher-trainer. He also collaborates with the University of Athens, Greece, planning and implementing intercultural and environmental projects. Like Joke Kypriotakis, he was on the editorial board for 'Sharing Practice in Intercultural Education' – (see above).

Tim Parke is Head of Linguistics at the University of Hertfordshire in Watford, UK.

Maria Pinzani Tanini now retired, was Head of International Relations at the Italian national association for teachers – the Centro d'Iniziativa Democratica degli Insegnanti in Rome.

Dr Wayne Thomas and **Dr Virginia Collier** are internationally known for their research on long-term school effectiveness for linguistically and culturally diverse students. **Dr Thomas** is a professor of evaluation/research methodology and **Dr Collier** a professor of bilingual/multicultural/ESL education in the Graduate School of Education at George Mason University in Fairfax, Virginia, USA. Currently, they are researchers with the national Center for Research on Education, Diversity and Excellence (CREDE), funded by the Office of Educational Research and Improvement of the US Department of Education.

Susan E Shaw is Head of the Equality Support Services for the Royal Borough of Kingston upon Thames, UK, managing education services for Travellers, Refugees and Bilingual learners and Equality of Opportunity across the Borough's Education and Leisure services and schools. She has been a member of the Intercultural Education Partnership since its inception and has spoken at symposia in the UK and across Europe, her paper on policy development being published by the IEP. Through her work with the IEP she has also been involved with special projects to address Street Children in Greece and Germany and is currently an honorary director and education advisor to a project in Berlin.

Introduction
'Learners' or 'Learned'?

Susan E. Shaw

Equality Support Services, The Royal Borough of Kingston upon Thames, UK.
Intercultural Education Partnership, UK

'In times of great change it is the learners who inherit the earth and the learned who find themselves equipped for a world which no longer exists.'

So said a speaker at a recent seminar in London, UK, on getting race equality onto the agenda. The collected papers in this book demonstrate the role of Intercultural Education Partnership UK in ensuring that we remain 'learners' and not the ill-equipped 'learned'.

There is no doubt that we are in times of great change. In Europe current and potential members of the European Union are having to cope with change arising from political re-structuring which has often resulted in displacement of vulnerable members of communities. Countries across Europe find themselves facing the challenges of welcoming and providing for new arrivals and how our societies respond to such changes highlights the weak spots and can engender feelings of unease, inadequacy or open hostility. The paper from Kostas Magos of Athens University looks at the experiences of such a displaced person and the consequences for his life chances as a result.

From North America the work of Wayne Thomas and Virginia Collier examines the impact that different types of language programmes have on ensuring equality – or inequality – of achievement for children who have English as an additional language (EAL/ ESL). Their research findings also challenge some of the misconceptions that policy makers have for the education of bilingual learners. Jim Cummins looks at the impact of their findings and his own earlier research with particular reference to literacy and considers the constant debate between 'phonics' and 'whole text' approaches. We ignore at risk his significant findings.

UK contributions begin with Constant Leung's chapter on Second Language Pedagogy. He looks at the ways that a majority language environment welcomes, teaches and supports minority language speakers and considers the impact that the perception of status of second language learning has on the way in which those language speakers are treated. Viv Edwards in England and Joke Kypriotakis in Rotterdam describe projects that involve bilingual parents as partners.

Tim Parkes' chapter on the learning situations of EAL learners and those by Anna Hirvonen of Finland and Maria Pinzani Tanini of Italy give voice to the practices of the many professionals working in the classroom.

England particularly is undergoing enormous changes in this field of education. Changes in special government funding arrangements are set to affect the educational and life chances of bilingual children in ways that cannot yet be predicted. Specialists in EAL and bilingual education and teachers and others working with ethnic and linguistic minority groups are anxious that the responsibility for their education may move from the hands of the 'learners' to the 'learned' – or more worryingly, to the 'unaware'. Carrie Cable provides practical suggestions for encouraging pupils to transfer their first language skills to their second and also ways to exploit the links between spoken and written understanding. The concluding chapter by Susan Jaine gives a refreshing view of the past and future provision for EAL pupils in UK schools.

The collection of these writings into one accessible publication will be of interest to anyone engaged in the education of bilingual children and learners from ethnic minority communities, whether they come to this for the first time or from long experience in the field;

be they policy makers or practitioners. Every contribution addresses not only the ways in which ESL/EAL is planned and delivered but also the climate in which this takes place.

The Intercultural Education Partnership UK has a long tradition of gathering together the latest research in the field and the views of professionals, and then disseminating them through networks, symposia and publications. Thus the wealth of local expertise that exists across Europe and beyond reaches a far wider audience. This book continues the tradition and I am at once proud and humble to have been involved with it.

Bringing together the writings of such eminent voices in this arena has been a personal journey through my involvement with the Partnership. I have been to the school in Gas Works Street in Athens and have met, if not Lefteris, then others in similar circumstances. I remember the smell of orange blossom wafting through the window as staff from the school gave up their weekend to impress their visitors from the UK, the Netherlands and Sweden by their dedication to address the difficulties they experienced and show the work they had done. They were embarrassed by their lack of resources, especially compared to those enjoyed by their visitors, whilst we in our turn were embarrassed by the fact that, despite all our resources, we were still confronting basically similar underlying problems of racism and inadequate understanding of the needs of bilingual learners. We wondered just how different our efforts might have been if we could have combined the resources from the visiting countries with the enthusiasm, dedication and energies of our hosts, most of whom have now moved away from Gas Works Street School – to the cost of the children.

I remember hearing Virginia Collier and Wayne Thomas at an IEP symposium presenting their initial findings about the length of time it takes a learner to develop cognitive fluency and the way in which failure to provide the learning conditions needed is tantamount to unintentional or institutional racism. At the same time they showed clearly that meeting those needs raised the achievement for *all* pupils. I remember returning to my own work fired by their research and implementing changes in the working practices in my own borough's language support service. Similarly, I doubt that there is now a school in the authority I work for that is not aware of the work of Jim Cummins that demonstrates the need to address the cognitive challenges of the curriculum through context-based work. After reading his new writing in this book, all I can say is 'Watch out literacy, your turn next!'

The work of the UK authors is similarly well known and has influenced how EAL teaching is approached. Their new contributions here give us an even more sound footing on which to build, wherever we are working and whatever our qualifications, interests or expertise. The collection of papers range from pedagogic to practical, from national research to small-scale classroom investigations, all grounded in the same beliefs in the rights of the child and equality of opportunity.

The importance of parents as partners has not been forgotten. The book includes just two from many interesting examples of the ways in which bilingual parents with little or no formal qualifications in the country of the writer, have been engaged in not only the education of their own children but, through the contribution of their language skills and other learned or natural competences, have also enriched the life of the school, raised the status of parents from the ethnic minority communities and supported the learning of monolingual children and parents.

In putting together these papers into one publication, the Intercultural Education Partnership is aware of the many other eminent practitioners that could have contributed. It is hoped that this book will inspire all who read it to develop their own expertise and share their knowledge with others – to remain learners ourselves but, more importantly, to ensure that the young people with whom we come into contact, directly or indirectly, succeed as learners. Only then can we have a future society fit for our children and children fit for our future society. A society where a future Lefteris can be proud to use his own name, be proud of his heritage and be seen as a valuable and included member of it. A society in which the linguistic rights and skills of bilingual children are recognised, celebrated, planned for and met because it is right so to do. A society that recognises and values diversity and difference as being part of the definition of society and not as in opposition to it.

This editorial would not be complete without recording special thanks to the directors of the Intercultural Education Partnership UK, Pam Gibbon and Stuart Scott, for their personal and untiring efforts to ensure that the expertise evident in this publication and through the work of the Partnership has kept multicultural and bilingual/EAL/ESL education firmly on the educational agenda.

Our thanks also to Trentham Books for the publication of these papers, thus making them available to a wide audience throughout the world.

Second Language Pedagogy: a value-free zone?

Constant Leung
School of Education, King's College London

Introduction

Across different parts of Europe, just as elsewhere in the world, the presence of ethnic and linguistic minority students in schools is becoming an everyday phenomenon. Schools and education authorities are increasingly faced with challenges concerning greater equality of opportunity and raising achievement for all. At the heart of these social and educational concerns lies a key pedagogic issue: the learning by and teaching of the majority/official school language (as a second or additional language) to language minority students for social and academic purposes.

The type of second or additional language (second language from now on) provision adopted by any educational system depends to a great extent on the way second language itself is conceptualised. Recent experience in some English-speaking countries has shown that broadly similar social goals – such as equal opportunities in education – can generate very different policies and curricula. The main purpose of this paper is to suggest an analytical perspective which makes explicit and visible the links between (often un-declared) assumptions about second language learning, language education policy and curriculum practice. Making the linkages visible makes it possible to formulate reflexive questions of a theoretical and empirical nature for the purpose of critical scrutiny. It is hoped that this analysis will contribute to the development of a more self-critical approach to the formation of policy and practice in second language education.

I

This chapter is organised in three main parts. First I briefly cite the second language curriculum provisions in England and the state of Victoria, Australia, to illustrate the differences that can exist. Next, I try to use Bernstein's (1996) linked concepts of competence and performance to provide an analytical account of the relationship between assumptions about second language learning and aspects of policy and pedagogic practice. In the final section this analytical approach is used to examine instances of policy and practice. Some recent developments in England illustrate my arguments.

Curriculum Differences: Two Examples
• Second language as a diffused curriculum concern

The second language curriculum provisions in England and in the state of Victoria represent two interesting and contrasting examples of curriculum thinking. In England, English as a second/additional language (ESL or EAL) is not recognised as a discipline in its own right, there is no dedicated curriculum or learning outcomes specification for it.[1] With the possible exception of very short induction courses in some schools, all second language students are expected to learn English and the curriculum content in the mainstream classes at the same time. This arrangement has been generally understood as a non-controversial part of an inclusive educational policy which emphasises equality of opportunity and access. Second language is regarded as a supra-subject phenomenon; it is understood to be a teaching and learning issue but its existence is not given curriculum subject status. Hence, 'the teaching of English is the responsibility of all teachers' (SCAA, 1996, p.2). At the same time, the curriculum specifications and assessment norms for (the National Curriculum subject) English in effect serve both mother tongue English-speaking students and those still learning English as a second language. It is emphasised that

> English is the area of the curriculum in which students have the opportunity to learn English and learn about language in many ways ... Throughout the programme of studies for Key Stages 1-4 there are examples of work related to words and their meanings, to grammar, style and idioms, which are essential for the development of English (op.cit., p8)

Teachers concerned with second language are advised that effective planning 'ensures a range of language experiences, including different audiences and purposes ...' (op.cit., p.13).

Within this perspective a number of broad second language pedagogical principles have been observed at work:

> Learning is best achieved through enquiry-based activities involving discussion ... To learn a language it is necessary to participate in its meaningful use ... The curriculum itself is therefore a useful vehicle for language learning ... A main strategy ... for both curriculum learning and language learning is the flexible use of small group work ... (Bourne, 1989, p.63)

At the same time, teachers are encouraged to pay attention to the use of English by individual students:

> [b]y ... encouraging children to apply their personal and already acquired knowledge to solving group problems, and from observing their efforts in a collaborative situation, to identify and provide any support that might be needed by individual children to acquire curriculum concepts and the languages needed to express them (Bourne, 1989, p.64). (Also see Edwards and Redfern, 1992 chapter 3 for a discussion.)

There are two levels of action in this conceptualisation of second language pedagogy.[2] On the curriculum and lesson planning level the emphasis is on the use of highly active and interactive inquiry-based learning activities that are recommended for all students, as Bourne (1989) observes. At the classroom teaching level, the job of the teacher is to render learning activities understandable by providing contextual support, eg. the use of realia or visual representations, and to offer assistance with the English language where necessary so that students may engage with their learning activities. One of the consequences is that second language teaching approaches have tended to prioritise active student participation in the learning processes and activities; at the same time the purpose of learning activities tends to be driven by the subject content curriculum. There is relatively little discussion about what language should be learned – a detailed second language curriculum specification of discursive and grammatical features is virtually unheard of. This lack of an explicitly formulated content agenda for second language teaching and learning has made consistent and credible assessment of language learning outcomes difficult, if not impossible. Yet this conception continues to underpin much of the national and local policy and practice discussions. For instance, teachers are advised that effective ESL teaching, inter alia:

- ensures a range of language experiences, including different audiences and purposes. This might include pupils talking with others in different classes, working with pupils more fluent in English ...

- makes use of variation in teaching styles, including direct instruction and one-to-one tuition, which offers pupils learning EAL opportunities for concentrated listening, as well as participation in group talk ... (SCAA, 1996:13).

On curriculum planning, Travers (1999:7) suggests that teachers ask themselves:

- Do I plan clearly defined and staged tasks which are purposeful, practical and geared towards the pupil's experience?

- Do I plan for collaborative work with visual and contextual support?

School inspectors are provided with a set of criteria to evaluate the quality of teaching. In schools and classes which have ESL students, the ESL-specific criteria for both primary and secondary include:

- the opportunity for, and quality of, speaking and listening

- the provision of effective models of spoken and written language

- how far the teaching helps EAL pupils to feel welcomed, confident and valued

- whether the content takes sufficient account of concepts, vocabulary and language register

- whether the selection of visual aids is both culturally relevant and of a high quality. (For secondary phase OFSTED, 1999:3; for primary phase OFSTED, 1998:64.)

Thus it can be seen that when second language is conceptualised as a diffused curriculum concern within a broad policy position of equality of access, there is a tendency to conduct pedagogic discussion in terms of inclusive general classroom practices.[3]

• Second language as a distinct curriculum focus

But second language pedagogy need not be conceptualised in a diffused way. The second language curriculum, known as the English as a Second Language (ESL) Companion (Board of Studies, 1996) in Victoria, Australia illustrates a different conceptualisation within a broadly similar educational policy committed to equality of opportunity for all students. The ESL Companion extends the English Curriculum and Standards Framework (CSF), which is an official state curriculum outcomes statement for English in primary and secondary schools. The Companion confers a curriculum identity on second language; on page 1 it 'recognises the need to control English language input, and systematically and explicitly teach English language skills to ESL students before the outcomes of the English CSF will be appropriate for them'. Student development is set out in three groups of broad stages of schooling for lower primary, middle and upper primary and secondary phases and there are clear outcome statements for each stage. For instance, at the end of Stage 2 in the secondary phase:

... a student will be able to

> Use and respond to the linguistic structures and features of some social and school-based texts and extend their application to some unfamiliar texts.

This will be evident when, for example, the student:

In a controlled context ... uses and responds to compound or complex utterances ...

In an uncontrolled context ... uses some cohesive devices to link ideas in utterances, eg. personal pronouns (it, she, they), demonstrative pronouns (this, these, those) ... (op.cit., p.95)

The distinctive ESL learning specifications for these three groups are structurally linked to the mainstream English CSF outcomes; as ESL students progress beyond the statements in the Companion teachers can use the mainstream outcomes to describe their language learning.

The state of Victoria is not alone in adopting this approach. Earlier nation-wide policy and curriculum discussions within Australia have pointed to the need to be explicit about ESL as a discipline and as a curriculum provision (Campbell and McMeniman, 1985; Curriculum Corporation, 1994, among others). This explicit recognition of second language as a distinct issue is clearly reflected in the terms of reference of a nationally funded research project on second language development (McKay, 1992, p.1):

The ESL Development Project's brief was to work towards:

• an increased capacity to measure proficiency development

• a better understanding of the interrelationship between mother tongue/English as a Second Language/English Language development issues

• assistance to teachers in maximising effectiveness of instruction for students of non-English speaking background

On ground level this explicitness has led to developments and formalisations of a variety of curriculum practices, such as in-class ESL support and specialist tuition at intensive English centres (Davison, 1995). There is clearly an acceptance that linguistic diversity and second language issues cannot be adequately addressed by a policy of 'a common pedagogy for all'.

Conceptualising the Nature and Process of Second Language Learning: Bernstein's Competence and Performance

These two contrasting second language curriculum provisions have been developed in social environments which subscribe, at least at a rhetorical level, to broadly similar social and educational goals of equality of opportunity and high achievement. The actual differences in curriculum practice are clearly bound up with specific historical and political circumstances. Analytically these differences can be understood in terms of Bernstein's (1996) linked concepts of competence and performance, which can illuminate the underlying characters of the current conceptualisations of second language pedagogic practices in schools. These concepts are not representations of actual policies or models of practice; they are abstracted values and beliefs on which actual policies and practices are based. In other words, they are ideological in nature.

Competence, as an abstract concept, is characterised as follows.[4]

- it is 'intrinsically creative and tacitly acquired' (Bernstein, 1996, p.55)

- it is a 'practical accomplishment' (loc.cit.)

- it is socially constituted through negotiation, in the broadest sense of 'social order as practice, cognitive structuring, language acquisition' (loc.cit.) and such negotiations are not culture specific (or exclusive) – everyone may participate

- its acquisition is not subject to the influence of the power differentials between participants.

Bernstein argues that there is a social logic in this concept of competence – a set of founding assumptions which shape and form the concept. In terms of second language issues, Bernstein's statements can be interpreted to include the following:

- All second language students can achieve and acquire this universally available and accessible competence; there are no inherent 'deficits' (p.56) in the students; age and other individual personal characteristics are not regarded as salient in terms of outcome; different first and second language developmental trajectories and pathways are not regarded as significant in terms of classroom level pedagogy

- The student is active in creating meaning and is creative in the use of current knowledge or resources, for example, using limited set of syntactical rules to create new meaning, irrespective of contextual differences; there is some sort of invariant approach to acquisition and use

- The acquisition is tacit and immanent; it is 'not advanced by formal instruction' nor is it subject to 'public regulation' (p.56) such as a subject syllabus; only facilitation and con-text management are required

- Acquisition of competence does not require or involve hier-archical power relations among the parties concerned; by extension, social class, ethnicity, gender, age as well as institutional positions may be acknowledged, but they are not actively formulated as constitutive elements of peda-gogy

- The present tense is the 'temporal perspective' (p.56); the past and the future are revealed through the moment of realisation and use; starting positions and learning out-comes do not bear on pedagogy or acquisition in any ex-plicit way.

This particular interpretation of competence can be contrasted with what Bernstein refers to as performance. He glosses performance in relation to primary school pedagogy as a practice (in the British con-text) which '... places ... emphasis upon a specific output of the acquirer, upon a particular text the acquirer is expected to construct, and upon the specialised skills necessary to the production of this specific output, text or product' (pp.57-58). Indeed, by construing the opposite of the above discussion on competence, one may extend this general characterisation to suggest a 'social logic' of performance for second language in the following way:

- All may enter into the development process but the outcome depends on numerous considerations including types and contexts of educational provision, age and context of learning, types/definitions of language attainment, background educational experience, individual differences in aptitude, cognitive style and motivation (August and Hakuta, 1997; Davies *et al*, 1997; Dörnyei, 1998; Ellis, 1994; Skehan, 1998; Spolsky, 1989; Thomas and Collier, 1997 among others); first and second language learner differences are not ignored; automatic universal outcome is not assumed

- There is variability in the use of language by learners. Such variability may be influenced by many factors, such as conditions of language use and types of task (Foster, 1998 among others) and form-function relations (see Ellis, 1994, chapter 4 for a general summary)

- Explicit teaching and conscious analysis have a role in second language development (Spolsky, 1989; Schmidt, 1990, among others); language learning is not always tacit – there is a role for noticing and hypothesis-testing (Swain, 1995; cf. Truscott, 1998)

- The distinction between the non-problematised notion of mother tongue (as a norm) and second language suggests one dimension of power differential and, in the context of formal teaching and schooling, the teacher-learner distinction suggests another (Cummins, 1996). The unequal inter-ethnic and inter-communal relations between majority language and minority language communities within the context of 'official' social integration may be yet another dimension of power differential (Bourdieu, 1991; Tosi, 1996)

- Second language development is seen as a process of progressive approximation towards the ideal, the benchmark or

> the norm, so there are stages or a sequence of learning. All second language/ESL scales (indeed any norm or criterion referenced scale for any subject) make the assumption that at any one point learners may show shortfalls (as measured against the expected achievement)

This performance-oriented characterisation of second language provides us with an alternative conceptualisation. It corresponds closely with current thinking in the specialist field of second language in countries such as Australia which have a less diffused view of second language than is apparent in England (Lo Bianco, 1998; McKay, 1998).

For the purpose of this discussion, the key differences between competence and performance can be summarised as follows:

Concept	Competence	Performance
Aspect of social logic (assumptions)		
1. Recognition of individual/group differences in acquisition pathways and outcomes	ø	+
2. Variations in styles/manners of acquisition and language use	ø	+
3. Explicit pedagogy and curriculum	ø	+
4. Hierarchical/unequal power relationships	ø	+
5. Development measured in stages/ outcomes	ø	+
Keys: + = salient; ø = not salient		

'Social Logic', Policy and Practice: an Analytical Perspective

By making the 'social logic' visible we can begin to explore the inter-connections between different parts of policy and practice that flow from a particular conceptualisation. The five aspects of social logic, whether in neat competence-only or performance-only forma-tion (or in different combinations of both), can be seen as constituent parts of an ideological basis of a policy and practice in support of social goals.

If policy and practice are not 'natural' or value-free, then it is no longer theoretically and empirically justifiable simply to scrutinise any policy or practice within the confines of its own terms of reference. For instance, if the key officially supported criterion for the quality of science or French language education is expressed in terms of the amount of instructional time devoted to these subjects, then a school with a large number of science and French lessons on its curriculum can claim to be offering a high quality education in these subjects. This we know to be but one of many possible measures. *Time spent on reading practice.*

Drawing on Bernstein's notions of competence and performance, we can begin to puncture the seemingly coherent articulation of dif-ferent aspects of policy and practice and to question policy assump-tions in a principled manner. To return to our earlier discussion, a competence-oriented policy and practice, which the current situation in England exemplifies, tends to assume universal learning capacity and developmental pathways. This assumption then legitimises a view of common pedagogic content and process for language learners of diverse backgrounds. In addition, it lends argumentative support to the use of a set of universal outcome statements or com-mon rating scale by which to measure attainment (OFSTED, 1997, p.2):

> The advent of the National Curriculum introduced a common assess-ment programme for all pupils, including bilinguals, through which their language competence could be mapped using the NC English levels. This has called into question the need for the continued use of

the pre-existing [second] language scales rather than relying upon the
NC English levels.

The self-referencing nature of this line of reasoning is clear. This
edifice of mutually supporting arguments is founded on a set of
assumptions which can be critiqued. The increasing evidence that
second language is associated with a range of divergent curriculum
attainment and language development pathways in different contexts
(August and Hakuta, 1997; Gillborn and Gipps, 1996; among
others) casts serious doubt on any assumptions of universal processes and outcomes. These assumptions are at odds also with the
increasingly performance-oriented policies in the wider educational
environment in England. The National Literacy Strategy (DfEE,
1998) and the call for setting of pupils in differentiated teaching
groups according to levels of achievement (OFSTED, 1999a) bear
witness to this tendency.

The same analytical perspective can be applied to a performance-
oriented policy and practice. This orientation assumes, for instance,
that first and second language development pathways are divergent
and that they are accompanied by different manners of acquisition;
such an assumption would also lead on to the argument for different
outcomes statements for different types of language learners. There
is, however, some indication that young (pre-literate in first language, primary school age) second language learners may mirror the
developmental behaviours of English mother tongue speakers in
spelling and writing (*First Steps – the Highgate Project*, undated).
This shows that there is a need to question some of the basic assumptions of the performance orientation. At the very least it suggests that
a performance-oriented view of divergent second language developmental pathways may need to be modified in terms of different age
ranges and first language knowledge.

This somewhat paradoxical situation, which suggests neither the
competence orientation nor the performance orientation, can adequately account for the complexity of second language development
is indeed instructive. Second language development in school contexts is a multi-dimensional and dynamic phenomenon which cannot

be adequately addressed by static monolithic assumptions. (For a further discussion see Valdés, 1997.) Nothing can be taken for granted. A policy position, if unchallenged, can be, at least for a time, reified and it can form networks of ideas and practice which Kuhn (1962/76, p.46) might refer to as community paradigms in which '[members of the professional community] work from models acquired through education and ... exposure to the literature often without quite knowing or needing to know what characteristics have given these models the status of community paradigms. And because they do so they need no full set of rules'. In other words, for as long as such a paradigm predominates, it assumes an air of naturalness which requires no further critical theoretical and empirical scrutiny. In such circumstances there is tendency for professional discussion to concentrate on refining and improving practice within the parameters of the prevailing policy discourse. A truly self-critical and reflexive approach to second language pedagogy, or indeed any pedagogy, requires us to engage consciously with analysis by disconnecting the articulated and disestablishing the accepted.

This discussion has suggested that the pedagogical assumptions and claims built on a particular policy should be critically examined with reference to actual experience, research and evidence of student achievement. This way we may stand a better chance of developing a student-focused second language policy and making real connections with the language needs of our students at both curriculum and individual levels. In the case of a competence-based ESL policy (as in England), some of the questions that teachers grapple with daily and which need to be addressed include:

- To what extent can we justify a second language policy (and its associated practices) which is mainly concerned with practical engagement with English (SCAA, 1996; OFSTED 1998 and 1999) in the context of curriculum activities? What role, if any, does teaching play? What attention, if any, do we pay to the complex relationships between the content of the curriculum and second language development?

- To what extent can we assume that second language students are tabula rasa when they engage with the use of English?[5] To what extent can we assume a 'universal' developmental pathway for all second language learners? What attention, if any, should we pay to issues such as individual learning experience (including first language learning), learning styles, and power relationships (such as race, ethnicity, gender, socio-economic status and age) in the classroom?

Notes

1   The term 'additional' language is preferred in England; at present one tends to find 'English as an additional language' (EAL) in official curriculum documents, rather than ESL. The term second language is used here because of its wide use in the international literature.

2   Virtually all official policy and curriculum statements acknowledge that the use of minority students' first language may help promote second language development, although there has been little support for this in England in terms of teacher education or curriculum provision.

3   There is a range of positions within this broad tendency; some are more second language (and language) conscious than others. For instance, the London Borough of Hounslow, produces a series of second language teaching guidance booklets for subjects such as history and geography; the advice is embedded within the mainstream classroom context.

4   Note that Bernstein is using the terms 'competence' and 'performance' in a very different sense than the one adopted in a great deal of the recent discussion in vocational education, which tends to regard competence as comprising a much more bounded and technically defined set of knowledge and skills or behaviours. For a discussion see Bates, 1995; Gonczi, 1994; Jones and Moore, 1995 among others. It should also be noted that these terms have been used differently in applied linguistics. For an example see McNamara, 1996, chapter 2.

5   There is acknowledgement of bilingual students' knowledge and skill in their first (or another) language. The point here is that this acknowledgement does not seem to have been incorporated into official statements on classroom pedagogy.

Accelerated Schooling for All Students:
research findings on education in multilingual communities

Wayne P. Thomas and Virginia P. Collier
George Mason University, Fairfax, Virginia. USA

As we educators prepare our students for the 21st century, we are aware of many changes occurring globally. Population mobility continues throughout the world at an all-time high in human history, bringing extensive cross-cultural contact among diverse language and cultural groups. Predictions focus on an increasingly interconnected world, with global travel and instant international communications available to more and more people. Businesses and professions seek employees fluent in more than one language, to participate in the international marketplace as well as to serve growing ethnolinguistic minorities living within each community. Students who graduate with monocultural perspectives and knowing only one language will not be prepared to contribute to their societies (Cummins in Ovando and Collier, 1998).

This chapter examines schooling in diverse contexts in the United States, with the goal of sharing insights for schools in the United Kingdom and Europe. During this century, US schools have not overcome enormous equity gaps between middle-class native-English-speaking students and those students who enter the schools with no proficiency in English. Ethnolinguistic minorities of many different language backgrounds are among the lowest achievers in American schools. It has been common practice to forbid these students to speak their native language in school and to teach them in separate classes while they are learning English, or to keep them in mainstream classes with just a little support from English as a

Second Language (ESL) specialists. These practices, we have found, have not worked well.

Our research has examined many different types of school programs provided for students in all regions of the US. Over the past fifteen years, we have conducted research in twenty three school districts in fifteen states, with over one million student records collected from 1982 to the present (Collier, 1989, 1992; Collier and Thomas, 1989; Thomas and Collier, 1997a, 1999b). We now have clear long-term student achievement data that unravels some of the mysteries sur-rounding the schooling of these students. Our data analyses from many school districts in diverse regions clearly show that enrichment bilingual programs that accelerate student learning are among the most promising models for schooling. Furthermore, these same programs are dynamic models for school reform for *all* students. When native-English speakers in US schools have the opportunity to receive schooling through two languages, where they have same-age peers to serve as peer teachers, they not only develop a deeper pro-ficiency in the new language but also accelerate their own academic growth. We will devote most of this chapter to the factors that promote acceleration of school achievement for students who begin their schooling with no proficiency in the language of the school. In the end the reader will see that these factors also apply to all students, majority and minority.

How Long?

Since 1985, we have been asking the research question 'How long?' as we analyze many data sets from different school districts. This question addresses the length of time required for students being schooled in their second language to become academically com-petitive with native speakers of the school language. Jim Cummins (1981) conducted the first published study addressing this question, analyzing the school records of 1,210 immigrants who arrived in Canada at age 6 or younger and at that age were first exposed to the English language. Cummins found that when following these students across the school years, with data broken down by age on arrival and length of residence in Canada, it took at least five to seven years, on the average, for them to approach grade-level norms on school tests that measure cognitive-academic language development in English. However, many US school administrators are extremely sceptical that five to seven years are needed for the typical immigrant student to become proficient in academic English. Furthermore, many policy makers still insist that there must be a way to speed up the process, stating that schools have just not done a good job and can do better. We became intrigued with the acerbic debates on this issue and decided that more research needed to be conducted on the 'How long?' question. More than a decade later, we have some clearer expansions for school administrators and policy makers.

Many measures for academic success are used in US schools that could potentially answer the question 'how long?'. Teacher-made tests examine ongoing progress, resulting in a grade for each subject or category of assessment at the end of each grading period. These grades are an important diagnostic measure, but the standards vary from teacher to teacher and cannot be generalized beyond the classroom level. Some school districts use locally developed tests to measure students' growth in each subject area, following district-wide objectives or competencies for each grade level established by curricular teams. These local tests help individual schools compare their performance to other schools in the same school district, but they cannot be generalized beyond the district level. Many states have developed standardized tests, based on statewide objectives or competencies that are required for all students in each state, but these cannot be generalized beyond the state level. Norm-referenced tests based on general curricular standards across the US for each grade level and normed on students nationwide provide the most generalisable and the highest difficulty measure of student achievement. These tests are usually commercially developed, and many states set standards that include testing students on one of these norm-referenced tests, commonly at Grades 4, 6, 8 and 11. (In the American constitution, education is a duty reserved to the individual states, not the national government, so there are no official national curricular standards or national testing requirements.) In our research, we use the national norm-referenced tests as the ultimate measure, a very challenging standard. These measure typical performance of native-English speakers across the country in all subject areas. Students' performance on this type of measure in Grade 11 is strongly correlated with their success in continuing with university studies when they graduate from high school.

Not all students choose to continue their education at university level, but we take the position that all students should have the opportunity if they so desire. Equal educational opportunity is a basic right in the United States, guaranteed by federal legislation and court decisions, but not all groups in the US have achieved educational success. When students of one ethnolinguistic background consistently score low throughout their schooling on the measures of educational achievement, then schools have under-served these students. Something is wrong.

Our operational definition of equal educational opportunity for US students with no prior background in English is this: The test score distributions of English language learners (known also as English as an Additional Language or EAL pupils in the United Kingdom) and native-English speakers, initially quite different at the beginning of their school years, should be *equivalent* by the end of their school years as measured by on-grade-level tests of all school subjects administered in English. This does not mean that every individual student must be on grade level. There will always be some high scorers and some low scorers among both the English language learners and the native-English speakers. But when these two groups of students are compared, the averages and variation of their test score distributions should be equivalent by the end of their school years. Our 'how long?' question examines the length of time required for these distributions to become equivalent and what influences students' success in reaching this point.

Confirming Cummins' (1981) research, we have also found that reaching parity with native-English speakers takes a long time. But politicians and laypersons assume that the only thing English language learners have to do is to become fluent in English, which is commonly thought to take about one or two years. Linguists and educators strongly disagree, pointing out that primary language acquisition is a process that takes from birth until young adulthood to acquire the full adult system of oral and written language across many contexts of language use and that second language acquisition is an equally complex developmental process that takes time.

However, the main point that policy makers need to understand is that for the school-age child, proficiency in the language of the school is only one of many, many processes occurring simultaneously. With every year of school, each student is experiencing intense academic, cognitive, linguistic, social, emotional, and physical development. This development is measured by the school tests, which examine cognitive growth as well as vocabulary and concept knowledge in English, applying this knowledge through problem-solving across the curriculum – mathematics, science, social studies, language arts, and literature. Language proficiency tests do not adequately measure language use in a school setting. But the school tests do, because they also measure age-appropriate language use at school, including the expanded knowledge acquired with each year of schooling. For example, with each year of school, to stay at the 50th percentile, typical students must make ten months of achievement gain on the tests given across the curriculum.

English language learners (ESL/EAL) are not generally given the norm-referenced school tests in English during the first one to two years after their arrival, since these tests will underestimate what the students actually know but cannot yet demonstrate in English. But after around two to three years of schooling in the US, these tests are given to EAL learners as well as all other students. We have found that, as a group, ESL learners typically score around the 10th to 11th percentile when tested on grade level and in English. That is a 40-percentile gap (equivalent to about 1.3 standard deviations) with typical native-English speakers nationwide, whose average score is at the 50th percentile. To close that large 40-percentile gap, ESL learners must accomplish more than one year's achievement for a number of years in a row. More specifically, they must make fifteen months of progress for each ten months of progress that the native-English speaker is making each year of school, and they must do this for six consecutive years to eventually reach the 50th percentile – a dramatic accomplishment! This is true for any 'at risk' group of students who initially score low on a norm-referenced test.

The vital thing for policy makers to recognize is that the native-English speaking students are not sitting around waiting for EAL pupils to catch up with them. While ESL pupils are acquiring English, the native-English speakers are forging ahead, making enormous progress with each school year in all school subjects as well as English language development and demonstrating their cognitive, linguistic, academic, social and emotional growth in the school tests. So we must help ESL learners not only to acquire the English language but also to *accelerate their academic growth* beyond that of typical native-English speakers. We have found that it is impossible to expect groups of even the most gifted bilingual students to accomplish this incredible feat in less than four years (the shortest time we have seen). Most ESL learners attending quality enrichment schooling programs that accelerate their growth take five to seven years – the same time period as Cummins found.

School Program Influence on Long-term Student Achievement

Sadly, we have found that typical school programs across the US have not succeeded in closing the achievement gap from the 10th to the 50th percentile. The large majority of ESL learners in the US are graduating around the 10th percentile and significant numbers are leaving school without completing a high school degree. Teachers often say, 'But my students are making great progress,' and they are. When a student first tests at the 10th percentile and completes school at the 10th percentile it means that the student has made tremendous growth, keeping up with the pace of the typical native-English speaker; making ten months of academic progress with each ten-month year of school, but not closing the gap at all. To become competitive with typical native-English speakers who are achieving at the 50th percentile, *former ESL learners must achieve sub-*

stantially more than ten months of academic progress for at least five to six consecutive years. A student graduating at the 10th percentile has little chance to enter university study and his/her educational opportunities are severely limited beyond high school.

Another pattern that we see in our data analyses is that ESL learners initially make dramatic progress. Whatever school program they attend; in the short term they appear to be closing the achievement gap, moving up to the 20th and then the 30th percentile in the first two to three years. But then as they leave their special program and enter the mainstream and as the cognitive and academic demands of the curriculum become greater at middle and high school (Grades 7-12), their percentile scores go back down to those of among the lowest achievers.

See Figure 1, Lines 4-5 and 6 for a visual illustration of this pattern. This figure presents student achievement in normal curve equivalents (NCEs), which represent a conversion from percentile ranks (with different amounts of achievement in each unit) to equal-interval scores. The 23rd-24th NCE is the 10th-11th percentile, which are the beginning and end-points of Line 6, representing those students who received one to two years of ESL pull-out when they first entered US schools in kindergarten. The three program types represented by Lines 4, 5, and 6, are among the most common in the US and the least successful in the long term. In these programs, students receive one to three years of assistance from specialists (bilingual and/or ESL teachers) and the remainder of their school years are spent in the mainstream.

But there are exceptions to this low achievement pattern, as can be seen in Figure 1. Some ESL learners are able to close the achievement gap by making fifteen months' progress with each year of school, reaching the 50th percentile in about six years and maintaining that high level of achievement or achieving still higher (as can be seen in Lines I and 2). These students will have many educational opportunities when they graduate from high school. Enrichment bilingual programs produce these exciting student outcomes. These programs are still uncommon in the US but are growing in number,

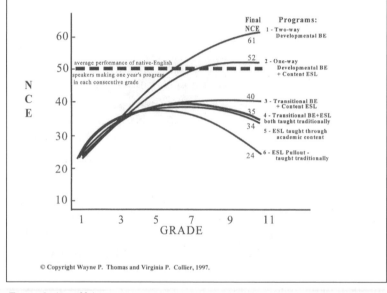

PATTERNS OF K-12 ENGLISH LEARNERS' LONG-TERM ACHIEVEMENT IN NCEs ON STANDARDIZED TESTS IN ENGLISH READING COMPARED ACROSS SIX PROGRAM MODELS

(Results aggregated from a series of 4-8 year longitudinal studies from well-implemented, mature programs in five school districts)
© Copyright Wayne P.Thomas & Virginia P. Collier, 1997

Program 1: Two-way developmental bilingual education (BE)
Program 2: One-way developmental BE, including ESL taught through academic content
Program 3: Transitional BE, including ESL taught through academic content
Program 4: Transitional BE, including ESL, both taught traditionally
Program 5: ESL taught through academic content using current approaches
Program 6: ESL pullout - taught traditionally

Figure 1. (.jpg file)

as educators work on school reforms and discover these models. In enrichment bilingual programs, students receive the mainstream curriculum through both their primary language and English, with challenging academic work that is cognitively on grade level. Teachers use cooperative learning, thematic interdisciplinary units, hands-on materials, and much work with video and microcomputers, as in any mainstream class. The materials and books present a cross-cultural perspective, and lessons activate students' prior knowledge for bridging to new knowledge. Enrichment bilingual classes for older students include problem posing, knowledge gathering, reflective thinking, and collaborative decision making.

Program Variations in the US

Of the distinguishing features influencing the dramatic differences in former ESL learners' long-term achievement, two factors stand out as especially powerful. One is the way the program is set up and perceived by staff – is it for remediation (ie to fix what is viewed as a problem) or for enrichment (ie to add to what the student already knows)? The second factor is the use of the students' primary language for instruction.

• *From Remediation to Enrichment*

Pull-out or separate bilingual and ESL classes generally have a stigma attached, because too often teachers focus on remediation and water down the curriculum, and the students know they are not being challenged with age-appropriate schoolwork. Initial assessment of the new arrivals focuses on what's missing and when students have little or no English, they are sent to a specialist to be 'fixed.' Even inclusion classrooms too often have the specialist (a bilingual or ESL teacher or 'aide' sitting at the back of the room tutoring students; whereas team teaching leads to more meaningful integration of students with varying proficiency in the language of instruction. Remediation in separate classes or in the back of the room most often results in lowered expectations and lower achievement for students. Furthermore, when ESL learners have no ongoing interaction with native-English-speaking peers, they have little opportunity for natural second language acquisition. Same-age peers are a crucial source of second language input. But they are beneficial only in settings that bring students together cooperatively and permit interactive negotiation of meaning and sharing academic tasks equally (Wong-Fillmore, 1991).

In contrast to remediation, bilingual enrichment classes provide quality, challenging, on-grade-level schooling through two languages in an integrated setting for all students. The strengths that ESL learners bring to the classroom, including knowledge and life experiences from other cultural contexts, as well as native-speaker knowledge of another language, are used as resources for learning, as essential building blocks. After enrichment bilingual classes are established, they are often perceived as classes for the gifted. Yet students of all levels of socioeconomic status and ethnolinguistic background and with varied levels of proficiency in the languages of instruction are able to flourish in these classes. Every class member is working on acquiring a second language, so all have an equally challenging task, including the native-English speakers who have chosen to enroll in the bilingual class.

- ### *The Power of Using Students' Primary Language for Instruction*

The second most powerful and positive influence on student achievement is to increase the amount of instruction in the students' primary language. ESL pull-out and ESL content alone (Lines 5 and 6 in Figure 1) are the two US programs with no primary language support. Graduates of ESL content programs significantly increase their achievement over graduates of ESL pull-out, from the 11th to the 22nd percentile. But by adding primary language support for two to four years in a well-taught bilingual class, which always includes ESL content, student achievement reaches a significantly higher level, the 32nd percentile (Line 3 in Figure 1).

Students in transitional bilingual classes are **closing** the achievement gap while they attend the program, but at the point where they are moved into all-English instruction, they continue 'to **keep pace** with the native-English speaker (making ten months' progress in each school year) but no longer are closing the gap. Whereas students who are placed in enrichment bilingual classes that focus on teaching the mainstream curriculum through two languages for at least six or seven years until the end of elementary school, are able to close the achievement gap in their second language and maintain their high performance (50th percentile or even higher) throughout the remaining years of their schooling.

We have found that groups of students who enter the program in kindergarten reach the 50th percentile on the school tests in their second language sometime between the 4th and 7th grade.

English-Only Programs

Figure 2 provides an overview of characteristics of the US school programs represented in Figure 1. In addition to the six program types, we have included in Figure 2 a theoretical description of Proposition 227 as specified in the referendum, approved by voters in the state of California in June 1998.

In actual implementation, California schools have varied greatly in their response to the Proposition, some following the guidelines closely, and others choosing to implement many variations, including bilingual schooling. We have no data on student outcomes for the program plan proposed by Proposition 227, but we would predict that its average long-term student achievement will be even lower than for ESL pull-out, since it has still fewer of the support characteristics of other program models. The programs presented here have greatly varying names from one school system to another, but we have chosen the most common terms used across the US.

• *ESL pull-out*

As can be seen in Figure 2, moving from left to right across the figure, the programs range from little or no support to strong support for students. ESL pull-out is generally carried out by an ESL resource teacher who receives ESL learners throughout the day for half, one or two hours, after which they return to their mainstream

Summary of Characteristics and Effectiveness
of Common Programs for English Language Learners

	REMEDIAL					ENRICHMENT	
	As in law	As well implemented				As well implemented	
While in these programs ➡ students receive:	Proposition 227 in California	ESL Pullout	ESL Taught Through Content	TBE with Traditional Teaching	TBE with Current Teaching	One-way DBE	Two-way DBE
Cognitive Emphasis	None	Little	Some	Some	Moderate	Strong	Strong
Academic Emphasis (in all school subjects)	None	None	Yes	Yes	Yes	Yes	Yes
Linguistic Emphasis L1=primary language, L2=English	Only Social English (only in L2)	Only Social English (only in L2)	Academic English (only in L2)	Develops Partial L1 + L2 Academic Proficiency	Develops Partial L1 + L2 Academic Proficiency	Develops Full L1 + L2 Academic Proficiency	Develops Full L1 + L2 Academic Proficiency
Sociocultural Emphasis C1=1st culture C2=2nd culture	None	Little	Some	Some	Moderate	Strong C1+C2	Strong C1+C2
Program Length	Transitory 1 year	Short-term 1-2 years	Short-term 2-3 years	Short-term 2-3 years	Intermediate 3-4 years	Sustained 6-12 years	Sustained 6-12 years
Native Language Academic Support	None	None	None	Some	Moderate	Strong	Strong
Exposure to English Speakers	No	Yes	Yes	No	Yes Half-day	Yes Half-day	Yes All day
Extra Instructional Cost	High (extra teachers needed)	High (extra teachers needed)	High (extra teachers needed)	Small-to-moderate (special curriculum)	Small-to-moderate (special curriculum)	Least expensive: Standard mainstream curriculum	Least expensive: Standard mainstream curriculum
Percent of Achievement Gap With Native-English Speakers Closed by End of Schooling (based on data- analytic research)	Presently un-researched but expect no long term gap closure or expect an increased achievement gap	None final average NCE scores equivalent to 11th national percentile	About one-fourth final average NCE scores equivalent to 22nd national percentile	About one-third final average NCE scores equivalent to 24th national percentile	About one-half final average NCE scores equivalent to 32nd national percentile	All of gap fully closed by end of school -- average scores at 50th national percentile	All of gap fully closed by end of school -- average scores above 50th national percentile

© Copyright Wayne P. Thomas and Virginia P. Collier, 1999.

Figure 2. (.jpg file)

class. Some schools have implemented ESL inclusion, in which the ESL resource teacher comes to the mainstream class and tutors the students for a time, helping to make the mainstream lessons more comprehensible. We include this as part of ESL pull-out, because the students only get this support for a limited period, and long-term achievement outcomes are similar. ESL pull-out is expensive because it requires extra ESL resource teachers (Crawford, 1997).

It is less effective because students miss important subjects while they attend ESL class; articulation with the mainstream teachers who send their students to ESL is difficult to maintain; and students have no access to primary language schooling to keep up with grade-level academic work while learning English (Ovando and Collier, 1998).

• *ESL content*

ESL content programs, also labelled sheltered instruction, provide much more support than ESL pull-out, because the ESL teacher is focused not just on teaching the English language but on teaching the entire curriculum. At middle and high school levels, ESL content staff team together to teach their strengths in curricular subjects. Sometimes a mainstream teacher teams with an ESL teacher when the ESL teacher is not certified in a particular subject. A well implemented ESL content program, taught during the first two to three years after the immigrants' arrival (with students gradually moving into the mainstream in Year 3), can raise former ESL learners' achievement to the 22nd national percentile by the end of schooling, which is much better than the 11th percentile for graduates of ESL pull-out.

This level of achievement (22' percentile) may be enough to allow admission to a community college, which can eventually lead to university study.

Remedial Bilingual Education
• Transitional bilingual education

This program provides half a day of ESL content teaching and half a day of instruction in the students' primary language in a self-contained classroom where students are all speakers of the same primary language (eg. Spanish). Students are gradually introduced to more instruction in English with each year until they are mainstreamed, typically after two to four years. This program model has been supported at state and federal levels, with extra funding provided for school districts that choose to apply. Some states such as Texas, Illinois, Massachusetts and New York passed legislation in the 1970s making this program mandatory for students who are not yet proficient in English when they enter school. In these states schools can also choose to create enrichment bilingual models, enhancing the transitional model if they wish.

Enrichment Bilingual Programs
• Two-way developmental bilingual education

The term 'two-way' refers to bilingual classes where two language groups are being schooled through each other's languages (eg. English and Spanish). This integrated model is a powerful one for school reform. We and other researchers have found that academic achievement is very high for all groups of participants, compared to groups of similar background who receive schooling only through English. This holds true for students of middle-class status and of low socioeconomic status, as well as African-American students and students of ethnolinguistic minority background (Christian, 1994; Collier, 1992; Lindholm and Aclan, 1991; Thomas and Collier, 1997a).

Some important implementation characteristics of two-way bilingual schooling include: a minimum of six years of bilingual instruction, focus on the core academic curriculum rather than a watered down version, quality language arts instruction in both languages, separation of the two languages for instruction, and use of the non-English (or minority) language for at least 50 percent of the instructional time and as much as 90 percent in the early grades. Also, a successful two-way program requires a positive bilingual environment that has full support of school administrators; a balanced ratio of students who speak each language (eg. 50:50 or 60:40, preferably not to go below 70:30, to have peer models for each language); promotion of positive interdependence among peers and between teachers and students; high-quality instructional personnel; and active parent-school partnerships. (Lindholm, 1990; Thomas and Collier, 1997b)

• *One-way developmental bilingual education*
The demographics of a given school community influence the feasibility of two-way programs. When there are insufficient native-English speakers enrolled, a one-way developmental bilingual program is an option, in which one language group is schooled through two languages. This model shares all the features of two-way-bilingual education and can be used in any school with large numbers of students of one primary language heritage. This enrichment model teaches the core academic curriculum through the students' primary language and the majority societal language in an intellectually challenging way, using students' linguistic and cultural experiences as a resource for interdisciplinary, discovery learning, The characteristics above for 'two-way' also apply to 'one-way'. (For more sources on the specifics of implementation of all of the programs discussed above, see Genesee, 1999; Ovando and Collier, 1998; Thomas and Collier, 1997b, 1999b.)

Current Approaches to Teaching
In our research we have found that some teachers use very traditional teaching methods while others have adopted teaching innovations of the last ten to fifteen years. We have found both types of teachers in almost all programs, so this factor, also influential, is a 'within-program' variation, rather than something that distinguishes one program from another.

In Figures 1 and 2 we provided one example for graduates of transitional bilingual classrooms. After attending a traditionally taught transitional bilingual class, student achievement outcomes, at the 24th percentile, were very similar to those for graduates of ESL content programs, at the 22nd percentile. Primary language support did not boost students' performance significantly in a traditionally taught bilingual class, whereas graduates of transitional bilingual classes taught with current approaches were at the 32nd percentile by the end of high school. This is a very significant difference.

We define traditional teaching as classes that are more textbook-driven and very teacher-controlled, allowing students few opportunities to interact with each other. In contrast, classes using what we call 'current approaches' focus on interactive, discovery, hands-on learning. Teachers in these classes often use cooperative learning, thematic interdisciplinary lessons, literacy development across the curriculum, process writing, performance and portfolio assessment, microcomputers, critical thinking, learning strategies, and global perspectives infuse the curriculum. In the two enrichment models – 'one-way' and 'two-way' developmental bilingual education – most of the teachers embrace current approaches, and ongoing staff development helps teachers to implement discovery learning across the curriculum.

Why Enrichment Programs Work Well

To accelerate students' academic growth, ethnolinguistic minorities need a school context that provides the same basic conditions that the majority group experiences. This includes attention to all the ongoing developmental processes that occur naturally – nonstop – for any child: *cognitive, academic, and linguistic* development in a supportive sociocultural context. We have created a model (Figure 3) which illustrates the importance of equal attention to these four dimensions of learning for students who come from a bilingual community.

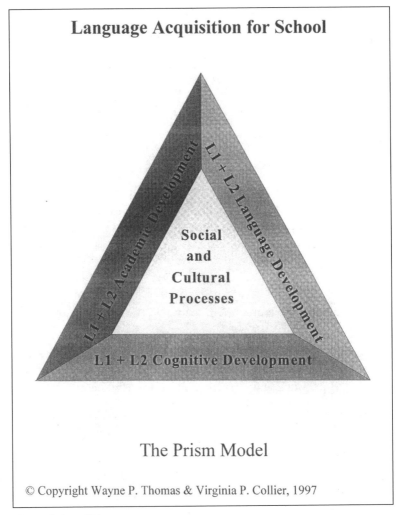

Figure 3. (.jpg file)

The four major components are interdependent and complex. If one is developed to the neglect of another, this may be detrimental to a student's overall growth.

For adult immigrants, second language is an appropriate first focus, because they are already cognitively and linguistically mature (including those not formally schooled). Thus, adults who learn a second language in a favourable sociocultural environment face a completely different endeavour than do children, who must make cognitive and academic progress while they are learning a second language. Consequently, programs that emphasize learning the second language as the main goal are appropriate for adults but cannot meet children's needs. Adult policy makers must remember this when making program decisions for children.

When students are given the opportunity to develop academically and cognitively through both their primary language and a second language, this accelerates their learning. But when students are denied use of their primary language in school, they lose several years of cognitive and academic growth while focusing on acquiring the second language, and we find that very few can make up the lost time (so drop out of school or graduate at the 10th percentile).

Sociocultural support is equally important. In schools with such support, ethnolinguistic minorities are respected and valued for the rich life experiences in other cultural contexts that they bring to the classroom. The school is a safe, secure environment for learning. Majority language speakers treat minority language students with respect, and there is less discrimination, prejudice, and open hostility. Minority students' primary language is affirmed, respected, valued, and used for cognitive and academic development. Families develop partnerships with the school and celebrate ongoing bilingual/bicultural learning in the community, for all ages.

For long-term success, ethnolinguistic minority students must receive the same benefits of a supportive learning environment that society automatically affords the majority language group.

Examining the Change Process

School policy makers have many decisions to consider in the process of school reform. Ethnolinguistic minorities are rapidly becoming a majority in many communities around the world, and schooling all students well leads to increased productivity and cooperative relations among all groups. It is in our own best interests to enrich our school programs so as to provide accelerated learning for **all.**

The following should be considered in school reform decisions:

1. The potential quality of program type

This refers to the power of a particular program's features to influence student achievement. Some of the programs discussed above are 'feature-rich', with enhanced potential to affect student achievement, while others are 'feature-poor', with little or no theoretical reason to believe that their use will help ethnolinguistic minority students to close the achievement gap.

2. The realized quality of program type

This is the degree of full and effective implementation of a program in terms of administrative support; teacher skills and training to deliver the full instructional effect of the program; and the degree to which program installation, processes and outcomes are monitored and formatively evaluated.

3. The breadth of program focus

This refers to instructional focus on the Prism Model dimensions of cognitive, academic and linguistic development to native-speaker levels in the second language as well as in students' primary language, in a supportive sociocultural school environment, as contrasted with a narrow and restrictive instructional focus, such as 'just learning enough of the majority language to get by.'

4. The quality of the school's instructional environment

This refers to the degree to which the school becomes an additive language-learning environment rather than a subtractive environment, including parental engagement and support of the instructional program. In an additive bilingual environment, students acquire their second language without any loss of their primary language. Students who continue to develop cognitively in their primary language and develop age-appropriate proficiency in both first and second languages can out-score monolinguals on school tests (Baker and Jones, 1998).

5. The quality of available instructional time

This is the degree to which instructional time is used effectively so that students receive maximally comprehensible instruction for an instructionally optimum time period, in classrooms where ethnolinguistic groups are not isolated, but where all students interact together and where instruction is driven by students' cognitive, academic and linguistic developmental needs.

Linguists know that more time in the second language is not necessarily better; the human brain can cope with only a few hours of intensive work in the new language in any one day. Thus primary language schooling for part of the day keeps students on grade level cognitively and academically and accelerates students' learning.

A successful program in the US allows average students who were ESL learners to out-gain average native-English speakers for four to seven consecutive years, so that the initial large achievement gap is gradually closed over time in all subjects and in English. This program must be 'feature-rich,' must be well implemented and delivered, must focus on all four of the Prism Model dimensions, must create an additive instructional environment in the neighborhood school, and must offer instruction that is fully comprehensible and appropriate for meeting students' developmental needs.

Such programs are rare in the real world. Most schools fall short on some or all of the above factors. However, it is vital that we realize that educators can create effective change by using these factors to design and implement programs. We only need the resources and the will to use them appropriately.

When we do this, ethnolinguistic minorities' school achievement will match or exceed majority students' achievement over time, achieving true equality of educational opportunity. As the number of under-served students continues to rise in most countries, our national productivity and welfare in the 21st century demands that we move away from polemics and toward action-oriented policies and accelerated education strategies that will dramatically improve the quality of education for all students.

Authors' note: For more information and research findings on enrichment bilingual education and other program models in bilingual/ESL education in the United States, visit the National Clearinghouse for Bilingual Education's website: [*www.ncbe.gwu.edu*] and the national Center for Research on Education, Diversity and Excellence's website: [*www.crede.ucsc.edu*]. Project 1.1 of the CREDE research, conducted by Drs. Thomas and Collier, addresses distinguishing curricular features of programs and the long-term academic achievement of English language learners who attended these programs. Findings from this new study will be reported in 2000-2001 on the CREDE website.

Learning to Read in a Second Language: Fact and Friction

Jim Cummins
University of Toronto, Canada

Two of the most volatile issues in contemporary educational debates in English-speaking countries concern

- appropriate ways of teaching reading to both English first language (L1) and English language learning (ELL) students, and

- appropriate ways of promoting overall academic achievement among ELL students.

This chapter addresses both of these concerns and outlines the current state of theory and research related to these issues and attempts to synthesize this theory and research in such a way that false oppositions are resolved and implications for practice are highlighted. I believe the research is consistent and fully interpretable when we leave aside the false dichotomies of 'phonics versus whole language' and 'bilingual education versus English immersion'. In fact, I argue that the same basic principles are operating when students are acquiring competence in comprehending and using the written code as are operating when students are acquiring the ability to understand and produce a second language.

The research outlined here relates to six issues that are central to policy and practice in these areas and then synthesizes the research within an instructional framework that permits its implications for classroom practice to be highlighted. The six issues are as follows:

- What developmental patterns are associated with acquiring different aspects of English language proficiency, specifically conversational and academic skills in English?

- What are the cognitive and academic consequences of bilingualism?

- What are the academic consequences of bilingual education for ELL students?

- What are the major instructional factors that contribute to the development of second language proficiency?

- What are the major instructional factors that contribute to the development of reading skills for all students and in particular for ELL students?

- How are cognitive and linguistic factors that operate within the individual student related both to affective variables and to the broader socio-historical context?

My overall argument is that we have a strong research basis for establishing coherent policies related to the education of bilingual/ELL students in general and to the teaching of reading in particular. However, this research basis has sometimes been obscured by the distortions of opposing positions that have been characteristic of debates in this area. A balanced approach is necessary not only in the classroom but also in the socio-political arena if the needs of students and the society are to be addressed effectively. The instructional framework that I will elaborate, on the basis of the research, suggests that we need to focus not only on technical aspects of teaching literacy and other academic content but, more fundamentally in the case of ELL students, on the human relationships that are established between teachers and students in the classroom. The ways in which identities are being negotiated in these human relationships will determine the extent to which students will engage academically or withdraw from academic effort.

Within the instruction itself, three foci should be apparent in any Unit or Lesson Plan. There should be a *Focus on Message, a Focus*

on Language, and a *Focus on Use*. These three foci are interconnected – if any one is omitted in the instructional process students'
literacy development is likely to be impeded. I try to show that they
provide a deep structure that resolves the apparent oppositions of
phonics versus whole language, and bilingual education versus
English immersion.

The Research Landscape
• *Conversational and Academic Proficiency*

Research studies since the early 1980s have shown that immigrant
students can quickly acquire considerable fluency in the target language when they are exposed to it in the environment and at school
but that, despite this rapid growth in conversational fluency, it
generally takes a minimum of about five years (and frequently much
longer) for them to catch up to native-speakers in their use of
academic language (Collier, 1987; Cummins, 1981b, 1984, Klesmer,
1994).

Collier's (1987) research among middle-class immigrant students
taught exclusively through English in the Fairfax County district
suggested that a period of five to ten years was required for students
to catch up. The Ramirez Report data illustrate the pattern (Ramirez,
1992): after four years of instruction, grade 3 Spanish-speaking
students in both structured immersion (English-only) and early exit
bilingual programs were still far from grade norms in English
academic achievement. By Grade 6, students in late exit bilingual
programs were beginning to approach grade norms. There are two
reasons why such major differences are found in the length of time
required to attain peer-appropriate levels of conversational and
academic skills. First, considerably less knowledge of language
itself is usually required to function appropriately in interpersonal
communicative situations than is required in academic situations.
The social expectations of the learner and sensitivity to contextual
and interpersonal cues (eg. eye contact, facial expression, intonation
etc.) greatly facilitate communication of meaning. These social cues
are largely absent in most academic situations that depend on knowledge of the language itself for successful task completion. In

comparison to interpersonal conversation, the language of text usually involves much more low frequency vocabulary, complex grammatical structures, and greater demands on memory, analysis and other cognitive processes.

The second reason is that English L1 speakers are not standing still waiting for English language learners to catch up. A major goal of schooling for all children is to expand their ability to manipulate language in increasingly abstract or 'decontextualized' situations. Every year English L1 students gain more sophisticated vocabulary and grammatical knowledge and increase their literacy skills. Thus, English language learners must catch up with a moving target. It is not surprising that this formidable task is seldom complete in one or two years.

With respect to the teaching of reading, some obvious implications can be noted: becoming an effective reader involves a long-term process of developing an awareness of, and ability to comprehend and use, highly complex aspects of language. In addition to the ability to use graphophonemic cues, fluent readers are required constantly to deepen their understanding of the semantic, syntactic, and discursive cueing systems embedded within written language. They cannot develop this degree of linguistic sophistication without immersion in a literate environment at school, especially if such an environment is not present in the home. However, they also require a strong instructional focus on language itself to demystify the complexities of written language and to alert them to the possibilities that literacy opens up for powerful self-expression – expression of their identities both to themselves and to others.

• The Positive Effects of Additive Bilingualism

There are well over 100 empirical studies carried out during the past 30 or so years that have reported a positive association between additive bilingualism and students' linguistic, cognitive or academic growth. The most consistent findings among these research studies are that bilinguals show more developed awareness of language (metalinguistic abilities) and experience advantages in learning additional languages. The term 'additive bilingualism' refers to the form of bilingualism that results when students add a second language to their intellectual tool-kit while continuing to develop conceptually and academically in their first language. (see August and Hakuta, 1997, and Hakuta, 1986 for reviews).

Bilinguals have a potential advantage in acquiring the kinds of metalinguistic insights that research suggests are important both for early reading skills acquisition and for more sophisticated academic language development. This has significant implications for teaching reading to bilingual/ELL students. One example relating to the role of cognates between L1 and L2 in developing academic language skills among Spanish speaking students will illustrate the point. Corson (1995, 1997) has pointed out that a large proportion of the words in written English text derive from Graeco-Latin origins; by contrast, the bulk of words that occur in everyday conversation derive from Anglo-Saxon origins. These words tend to be one or two syllables long and of high frequency, while the Graeco-Latin words tend to be two or three syllables long and of relatively low frequency. The point here is that this literary vocabulary in English text has many cognates in Romance languages such as Spanish and these cognates in Spanish tend to be more common words than they are in English, where they are specialized for specific kinds of literary or technical expression. Thus, Spanish-speaking students who have continued to develop their language and literacy skills in Spanish have at their disposal a first language database that potentially gives them privileged access to the most complex vocabulary in English.

However, research suggests that many Spanish-speaking students do not make optimal use of this potential resource (Nagy *et al.,* 1993). The obvious reason why they might not is that they have never been alerted to its availability or function by their teachers.

A final point with respect to vocabulary knowledge and the potential of cognates: countless studies have shown that vocabulary knowledge is the single best predictor of both reading and overall cognitive academic ability, as measured by typical IQ tests. Thus, a simple strategy of systematically focusing students' attention on the relationships between their implicit primary language knowledge and the structure of academic English could dramatically increase both reading performance in English and students' cognitive functioning in relation to written text.

- ### *Bilingual Education and the Interdependence of First and Second Languages*

I have argued for more than 20 years that the research on bilingual education from countries around the world is highly consistent in what it shows. Specifically, this research supports the notion that academic proficiency is interdependent across languages. The interdependence principle has been stated as follows (Cummins, 1981a):

> To the extent that instruction in Lx is effective in promoting proficiency in Lx, transfer of this proficiency to Ly will occur provided there is adequate exposure to Ly (either in school or environment) and adequate motivation to learn Ly.

The term *common underlying proficiency* (CUP) has also been used to refer to the cognitive/academic proficiency that underlies academic performance in both languages.

Consider the following research data that support this principle:

- In virtually every bilingual program that has ever been evaluated, whether intended for linguistic majority or minority students, spending instructional time teaching through the minority language entails no academic costs for students' academic development in the majority language. This is borne out in the review of research carried out by Rossell and Baker (1996) as well as by the 30 chapters describing an extremely large number of bilingual programs in countries around the globe in the volume edited by Cummins and Corson (1997).

- Countless research studies have documented a moderately strong correlation between bilingual students' L1 and L2 literacy skills in situations where students have the opportunity to develop literacy in both languages (for a detailed review of these studies see Cummins, 1991b). It is worth noting, as Genesee (1979) points out, that these findings also apply to the relationships among very dissimilar languages as well as to languages that are more closely related, although the strength of relationship is often reduced (eg. Japanese/English, Chinese/English, Basque/Spanish – see Cummins *et al.*, 1984; Cummins *et al.*, 1990; Cummins, 1983; Gabina *et al.,* 1986; Sierra and Olaziregi, 1989, 1991).

Fitzgerald's (1995) comprehensive review of US research on cognitive reading processes among ELL students concluded that this research consistently supported the common underlying proficiency model:

> .. considerable evidence emerged to support the CUP model. United States ESL readers used knowledge of their native language as they read in English. This supports a prominent current view that native-language development can enhance ESL reading. (p. 181)

By contrast, results were equivocal with respect to the timing of reading instruction in L1 and L2. No clear pattern of superiority emerged from the data.

Verhoeven's (1991) conclusion from his research with Turkish-Dutch bilingual students in the Netherlands illustrates the type of finding that has been observed in educational contexts throughout the world:

> With respect to linguistic measures, it was found that a strong emphasis on instruction in L1 does lead to better literacy results in L1 with no retardation of literacy results in L2. On the contrary, there was a tendency of L2 literacy results in the transitional classes being better than in the regular submersion classes. Moreover, it was found that the transitional approach tended to develop a more positive orientation toward literacy in both L1 and L2. ... Finally, there was positive evidence for ... [the] interdependence hypothesis. From the study on biliteracy development it was found that literacy skills being developed in one language strongly predict corresponding skills in another language acquired later in time. (p. 72).

Verhoeven's (1991, 1994) study shows that that, under certain conditions, transfer of literacy-related skills can occur both ways in bilingual programs: from minority to majority and from majority to minority languages. This pattern has also been reported in the context of early French immersion programs by Cashion and Eagan (1990). As students spontaneously acquired English reading and writing skills, they transferred this knowledge from English to French, a process that was much more evident than transfer of literacy-related skills from French to English.

A consistent finding comes from the California State Department of Education's (1985) 'Case Studies' project carried out in five schools, attempting to implement the theoretical framework development by the Department. Consistently higher correlation was found between English and Spanish reading skills (range $r=0.60$-0.74) than between English reading and English oral language skills (range $r=0.36$-0.59). It was also found that the relationship between L1 and L2 reading became stronger as English communicative skills increased ($r=0.71$, $N=190$ for students in the highest category of English oral skills). Similar findings were reported by Lee and Schallert (1997) in a study involving Korean school-aged students learning English as a foreign language. In this case, however, the relationship between English 'proficiency' and English reading was greater than between Korean reading and English reading.

In short, the research data show clearly that within a bilingual program, instructional time can be focused on developing students' literacy skills in their primary language without adverse effects on the development of their literacy skills in English. Furthermore, the relationship between first and second language literacy skills suggests that effective development of primary language literacy skills can provide a conceptual foundation for long-term growth in English literacy skills.

It is important to highlight what the research data is not saying in addition to what it is saying. The research data sketched here says nothing about whether L1 or L2 should be the initial language of reading instruction within bilingual programs, nor about the amount of time that should be spent learning through each language in the early grades. Nor does it say when English reading and language arts should be introduced within a bilingual program. The research is also largely silent as to whether there is any specifiable level of 'oral English' that students should have acquired before formal English reading instruction is introduced. On all of these issues, no definitive statements can be made since a variety of models appear to work well under different conditions.

My own interpretation of the data, on which I will elaborate later, is that these issues represent 'surface structure' issues that are much less central than 'deep structure' issues. These include the extent to which the school is making a serious attempt to promote students' L1 literacy (and awareness of language generally), and the extent to which the teacher-student interactions in the school are affirming of students' academic and cultural identities and strive to establish genuine partnerships with culturally diverse parents.

With respect to the role of students' L1, the research is very clear that for groups that appear to be at risk of school failure, promotion of strong L1 literacy makes a powerful contribution to students' academic success. In most bilingual programs for Spanish-speaking students, it will also make much more sense to introduce reading in L1 rather than in L2 for three reasons:

a) Spanish is the language students know best

b) it is generally considered much easier to acquire decoding skills in Spanish than in English because of the greater regularity of sound-symbol relationships, and

c) introducing reading in Spanish reinforces the affirmation of students' identity as a result of communicating to students and parents the importance of the family language and culture.

However, the same arguments may not apply as clearly to groups such as Chinese or Korean students because of the much more complex literacy system in those languages, which take even native speakers in monolingual contexts many years to acquire. Also, the potential advantages of introducing reading in L1 to Spanish-speakers should not blind us to the fact that other models that have introduced reading in L2 before L1 or in both languages in quick succession have also been successful (eg. El Paso Independent School District, 1992; Pena-Hughes and Solis, 1980). The central factor appears to be the extent to which the school is making a serious attempt to promote students' L1 literacy rather than the specific linguistic order in which reading is introduced.

• *Determinants of Second Language Acquisition*

Virtually all applied linguists agree that access to sufficient comprehensible input in the target language is a necessary condition for language acquisition; most applied linguists, however, also assign a role to

a) a focus on formal features of the target language

b) development of effective learning strategies, and

c) actual use of the target language (eg. Chamot and O'Malley, 1994).

Three aspects of 'comprehensible input' need to be highlighted. First, the extent to which input will be comprehended depends as much on the cognitive schemata or prior knowledge of the student as it does on the characteristics of the input in itself. A migrant student who has much informal background knowledge regarding harvesting plants and vegetables and associated conditions for adequate growth is more likely to understand an English science lesson on these topics than a lesson of equal linguistic difficulty on a topic s/he knows very little about. The more s/he understands, the more s/he learns, and the more background knowledge s/he builds up as a foundation for future learning. *The implication here is that a crucial component of effective instruction for bilingual/ELL students is the activation of students' prior knowledge, together with building background knowledge, to ensure that the cognitive schemata required for comprehension are in place.*

Second, it is clear from the data reviewed on the interdependence principle that background knowledge developed in students' L1 helps make input in L2 comprehensible. This suggests the importance of teachers finding a way to tap into and amplify students' background knowledge, particularly in English-only classroom situations where the teachers may not speak the languages of their students. *An implication is that teachers should encourage students to continue to develop their knowledge of the world and curriculum content in their L1 while they are acquiring English since this knowledge increases their cognitive power to comprehend and acquire English.*

Third, 'comprehension' is not an 'all-or-nothing' phenomenon; our understanding of words, stories or events deepens the more we relate them to our prior knowledge and personal histories, the more we critically analyze them with respect to their logic and social significance, and the more we express our developing understanding through creative action such as writing on a topic, dramatizing and reinterpreting events, etc. *Thus, the notion of 'Providing comprehensible input' should be interpreted as encouraging students to engage in a process of collaborative critical inquiry where issues are analyzed and discussed as a way of deepening understanding and motivating further inquiry (eg. through further reading).*

• *Reading Development in L1 and L2 Contexts*

The research on how to teach reading is far more consistent than might be apparent from the volatile debates that have raged on this topic. Part of the confusion derives from failure to distinguish the process of acquiring decoding skills from the process of deepening and extending students' abilities to comprehend and use written language. The confusion also derives from distortions of opposing views that almost inevitably occur when issues are hotly debated. For example, whole language advocates frequently constructed phonics and virtually any direct instruction of language or academic skills as 'the enemy'. Thus their message regarding the importance of focusing on meaningful engagement with text and encouraging extensive reading of a wide variety of linguistic genres frequently got lost in the acrimony. By the same token, those who strongly advocated explicit phonics instruction sometimes failed to acknowledge that whole language theory provided for considerable indirect instruction in phoneme-grapheme correspondences as well as other formal aspects of how the language worked. The debate has been further complicated by the gap that often exists between theory and practice and the fact that some whole language classrooms may have failed to provide sufficient focus on language (and particularly phonics) through either direct or indirect means.

I will examine the research separately for decoding and comprehension in order to highlight what is instructionally important.[1]

Decoding

The California Department of Education (1996) points out that 'Research has shown repeatedly that phonemic awareness is a powerful predictor of success in learning to read' (p. 4). They advocate systematic explicit phonics instruction 'where letter-sound correspondences for letters and letter clusters are directly taught; blended; practiced in words, word lists, and word families; and practiced initially in text with a high percentage of decodable words linked to the phonics lesson. Teachers should provide prompt and explicit feedback' (p.6).

Anderson *et al.* (1985) in the influential volume *A Nation of Readers*, express the importance of phonics instruction in a less definitive way:

> ... phonics instruction should aim to teach only the most important and regular of letter-to-sound relationships ... once the basic relationships have been taught, the best way to get children to refine and extend their knowledge of letter-sound correspondences is through repeated opportunities to read. If this position is correct, then much phonics instruction is overly subtle and probably unproductive. (p. 38)

Once again, there is probably no real contradiction between these different emphases. A few examples may make this clear.

Students who are immersed in a literate environment in the home can usually pick up decoding skills with minimal formal instruction in phonics. They usually need some initial help to 'break the code' but once they have done so they make rapid progress on their own by relating their knowledge of oral language to the written language. They know that there is payoff in print so they are highly motivated to become independent readers. An example comes from students in Canadian French immersion programs and English background students in two-way bilingual immersion programs. These students are introduced to reading instruction through their L2 in which, at the beginning of grade 1, they have relatively minimal fluency. English reading in these programs is not formally introduced until grade 2, 3 or sometimes even 4. It is almost invariably observed that shortly after students have developed some decoding skills in French (or Spanish), they spontaneously start decoding in English (their L1) and are usually much more fluent readers in English than in their L2 by the end of grade 1. They have had no phonics instruction in English but because of their immersion in a literate environment and the support for literacy in school they become highly fluent readers.

Similarly, ample experience in whole-language classrooms shows that students who have a strong literate background in the home typically develop strong decoding and comprehension skills in these classrooms. There is also documentation that students who may not have strong literate backgrounds in the home can often do well in such classrooms (eg. Edelsky, 1991).

However, it is equally clear that what Reyes (1994) has termed the 'one-size-fits-all' assumption of some whole-language programs is inappropriate for many students from culturally diverse and bilingual backgrounds. Delpit (1988) has argued this point most forcefully. She suggests that African-American inner city students require more explicit direct instruction and corrective feedback regarding the 'rules of the language game' than is the case in many whole-language classrooms.

In short, students vary widely in the extent to which they require and will benefit from an explicit focus on phonics to develop adequate decoding skills. Some who have been immersed in a literate environment in the home may require minimal formal instruction to start decoding whereas others who lack that exposure to print in the home may require much more direct and explicit instruction focused on phonics but also on many other features of language. It should not be forgotten that it is not only phonemic sensitivity that is related to early reading development but also the wider spectrum of language awareness that Marie Clay has termed Concepts about Print. Concepts about Print in both L1 and L2 have been found to be strongly related to English reading development among Portuguese background students in Toronto (Cummins, 1991a).

We should also not forget the importance of immersion in a literate environment that permits most middle-class students to acquire reading skills with relatively little difficulty. Phonics instruction for low-income students will be much more effective if we supplement it with the immersion in literacy both in the home and school that has repeatedly been shown to be a major determinant of reading development (eg. Wells, 1986). This is dramatically illustrated by the results of a two-year project carried out in six schools in an inner-city area of London, England, which showed major improvements in children's reading skills simply as a result of sending books home on a daily basis with the children for them to read to their parents, many of whom spoke little English and were illiterate in both English and their L1 (predominantly Bengali and Greek) (Tizard, Schofield and Hewison, 1982). The children attending the two schools that implemented the 'shared literacy' program made significantly greater progress in reading than a comparison group in two different schools who received additional small-group reading instruction from a highly competent reading specialist. Of particular importance is the fact that the differences in favor of the shared literacy program were most apparent among children who were initially having difficulty in learning to read. Both groups made greater progress than a control group in two schools who received no special treatment. Teachers involved in the home collaboration reported that children showed an increased interest in school learning and were better behaved.

The impact of this project in motivating students to read can be seen from the fact that the students in the two 'shared reading' schools exhausted the supply of books in the school libraries that were appropriate for early elementary grades simply because they read so much.

In short, for ELL students who do not come from a highly literate home environment, initial instruction should focus both on developing awareness of how the language works and inducting students into the world and the wonders of books both in school and, to the extent possible, at home. What this might look like in practice is illustrated by Goldenberg's (in press) description of a successful school-change project involving bilingual education for Latino/ Latina students where both 'bottom-up' and 'top-down' processes were applied. Among the former for kindergarten and grade 1 students were naming and recognizing letters, recognizing beginning sounds of words, hearing and discriminating rhymes, writing letters and words from dictation, and 'estimating' the spellings of words when they write (i.e. 'invented spelling' in whole-language parlance). Top-down strategies included reading or 'pseudo-reading' for pleasure, talking about books, and encouraging attempts at communicative writing.

Comprehension

It is probably appropriate to start with what is probably the largest study of reading achievement and instruction ever conducted. Postlethwaite and Ross (1992) in an evaluation of reading achievement in thirty two systems of education around the world showed that the amount of time students reported they spent in voluntary reading activities was amongst the strongest predictors (2nd) of a school's overall reading performance. The first ranked indicator was the school's perception of the degree of parent cooperation. This variable may be an index of socioeconomic status. The significance of reading frequency in promoting reading development is also evident from the high rankings of variables such as *Amount of reading materials in the school (8th), Having a classroom library (11th), and Frequency of borrowing books from a library (12th)*. With respect to teaching methods, a focus on *Comprehension instruction was ranked 9th and Emphasis on literature was ranked 17th, both considerably higher than whether or not the school engaged in explicit Phonics teaching (41st).*'

This does not mean that phonics instruction is not important in the early stages of learning to read. As indicated above, for many students it may be a crucial component. However, at higher levels of reading proficiency, phonics plays a lesser role in comparison to the amount of reading that students engage in and the amount of instruction they receive that is specifically focused on comprehension.

Consistent with these results, Fielding and Pearson's (1994, p. 62) review of research in this area highlights four components of a reading program that are strongly supported by the data:

- Large amounts of time for actual text reading

- Teacher-directed instruction in comprehension strategies

- Opportunities for peer and collaborative learning, and

- Occasions for students to talk to a teacher and one another about their responses to reading.

The power of reading to promote knowledge of the target language is supported in a wide variety of studies. Elley and Mangubhai (1983) for example, demonstrated that 4th and 5th grade students in Fiji exposed to a 'book flood' program during their thirty minute daily English (L2) class in which they simply read books either alone or with the guidance of their teacher, performed significantly better after two years than students taught through more traditional methods. Elley (1991) similarly documented the superiority of book-based English language teaching programs among primary school students in a variety of other contexts (see also Krashen, 1993, for a comprehensive review).

In a similar vein, Lightbown (1992), reported that elementary school students in New Brunswick in Canada, learning English as a second language through listening to tape-recorded stories and other material while following the written text with no formal teaching, learned at least as much between grades 3 and 6 as did students in a more traditional aural-oral program. Both programs lasted for half an hour a day and in the experimental program student autonomy was strictly respected insofar as there was 'no teaching, no testing, no probing students' comprehension' (p. 356).

In short, the importance of extensive reading for the development of vocabulary and other aspects of academic knowledge is over-whelmingly supported by the research. The only place students find the low frequency vocabulary required for academic progress is in texts. In reviewing this area, Corson (1997, p.677) points out that

> ... printed texts provided much more exposure to [Graeco-Latin] words than oral ones. For example, even children's books contained 50% more rare words than either adult prime-time television or the conversations of university graduates; popular magazines had three times as many rare words as television and informal conversation.

Similarly, Nation and Coady (1988), reviewing research on the relationship between vocabulary and reading, point out that voca-bulary difficulty has consistently been found to be the most signi-ficant predictor of overall readability. Once the effect of vocabulary difficulty (usually estimated by word frequency and / or familiarity and word length) is taken into account, other linguistic variables, such as sentence structure, account for little incremental variance in the readability of a text. They summarize their review as follows: 'In general the research leaves us in little doubt about the importance of vocabulary knowledge for reading, and the value of reading as a means of increasing vocabulary' (p.108). One example of the research demonstrating the extent to which vocabulary can be acquired from context is Nagy, Herman and Anderson's (1985) demonstration that the probability of learning a word from context after just one exposure is between 0.10 and 0.15. As learners read more in their second language, repeated exposure to unfamiliar words will exert an incremental effect on vocabulary learning.

In short, reading extensively in a wide variety of genres is essential for developing high levels of reading comprehension. This is particularly the case for ELL students since they are attempting to catch up to students who are continuing to develop their English (L1) academic language proficiency.

The important role that extensive reading itself plays in fuelling reading development does not mean that teacher directed instruction is unimportant. On the contrary, students will become more effective readers if they acquire efficient strategies for text interpretation and analysis and if the teacher directs their attention to how the language of text works (eg. the role of cohesive devices). This is illustrated by the strong showing of *Comprehension instruction* in the Postlethwaite and Ross (1992) study. Fielding and Pearson (1994) similarly rank 'teacher-directed instruction in comprehension strategies' second to 'large amounts of time for actual text reading' in their review of the implications of reading research for instruction (see Chamot and O'Malley, 1994, for a comprehensive review of the significance of learning strategies for ELL students' academic learning).

Wong Fillmore (1997) has articulated the role that teachers should play in making texts work as input for language learning:

- Provide the support learners need to make sense of the text

- Call attention to the way language is used in the text

- Discuss with learners the meaning and interpretation of sentences and phrases within the text

- Point out that words in one text may have been encountered or used in other places

- Help learners discover the grammatical cues that indicate relationships such as cause and effect, antecedence and consequence, comparison and contrast, and so on.

In short, teachers help written texts become usable input not only by helping children make sense of the text but by drawing their attention, focusing it, in fact, on how language is used in the materials they read. Done consistently enough, the learners themselves will soon come to notice the way language is used in the materials they read. When they do that everything they read will be input for learning. (1997, p. 4)

• *Academic Development in the Context of Status and Power Relations*

I have argued (Cummins, 1996) that academic success for ELL students is fundamentally determined by the processes of identity negotiation that are enacted within the classroom and school contexts and the extent to which these processes of identity negotiation actively challenge the devaluation of students' language and culture in the wider society. Instruction is effective only to the extent to which it generates academic engagement. Bilingual/ELL students are likely to withdraw rather than engage academically when their personal and cultural identities are devalued by school structures (eg. curriculum, assessment practices, language policies, etc.) and by the ways educators have defined their roles in relation to issues of diversity. Thus, regardless of how effective particular methods of teaching literacy or developing cognition are considered to be in the abstract, they will result in minimal student progress in situations where:

- students' language and culture cannot find expression within the classroom and school

- parents are excluded from participation as partners in their children's education

- instruction fails systematically to activate students' prior experience and support them (and their communities) in generating new knowledge, creating literature and art, and acting on social realities that affect their lives.

In other words, when the experiences and voices of students and communities are suppressed within the school, historical patterns of devaluation of lower status groups in the wider society are being replicated and reinforced in the interactions that educators, individually and collectively, orchestrate with their students in school. Learning under these conditions frequently entails a denial of self and rupturing of family bonds, as Richard Rodriguez' autobiography *Hunger of Memory* (1982) so vividly describes.

This perspective is very similar to that articulated by other theorists. As noted, Reyes (1992) and Delpit (1988) argue against the implementation of 'one-size-fits-all' whole-language methods that fail to take account of the cultural and experiential realities of culturally diverse students. Bartolomy (1994) argues against the 'methods fetish' that obscures the reality of the 'quasi-colonial nature of minority education. 'A humanizing pedagogy, by contrast,

> ... can serve to offset potentially unequal relations and discriminatory structures and practices in the classroom and, in doing so, improve the quality of the instructional process for both student and teacher. In other words, politically informed teacher use of methods can create conditions that enable subordinated students to move from their usual passive position to one of active and critical engagement. I am convinced that creating pedagogical spaces that enable subordinated students to move from object to subject position produces more far reaching, positive effects than the implementation of a particular teaching methodology, regardless of how technically advanced and promising it may be. (p. 177)

What is the empirical basis for highlighting issues related to power and status in the wider society and the ways in which these factors influence educator-student interactions in school? The empirical data have been extensively reviewed in many publications (see for example the special issue of *Anthropology & Education Quarterly*, Fall, 1997, edited by Margaret Gibson). However, two aspects of the data can be mentioned here. First, John Ogbu (1978) has drawn attention to the fact that issues of status and power in the wider society are strongly related to patterns of success and failure in school. The groups that experience the most persistent and widespread school failure in the United States and Canada have been subjected to a history of subordination and devaluation of their worth in the wider society over generations (eg. African-Americans, Native Americans, Latino/Latinas, Hawaiian-Americans in the US and First Nations [Native] Peoples, minority Francophones and African-Canadians in Canada). Similar patterns are evident in other countries, although the picture is considerably more complex than can be captured by Ogbu's distinction between voluntary minorities (who do well academically) and involuntary minorities (who do poorly academically).

Some of the ways in which these societal relationships of status and power play themselves out in the school context is suggested by the results of the extremely detailed ethnographic study conducted by Poplin and Weeres (1992) in four multi-ethnic schools in southern California. They concluded that:

> Relationships dominated all participant discussions about issues of schooling in the US. No group inside the schools felt adequately respected, connected or affirmed. Students, over and over again, raised the issue of care. What they liked best about school was when people, particularly teachers, cared about them or did special things for them. Dominating their complaints were being ignored, not being cared for and receiving negative treatment. (p.19)

Teachers in these schools reported that their best experiences were when they connected with students and were able to help them in some way. However, they also reported that they did not always understand students who are culturally different from themselves. They felt isolated and unappreciated inside schools by the students, administrators and parents as well as within the larger society.

A framework that attempts to connect the broader *macro-interactions* in the wider society with the *micro-interactions* going on between educators and culturally diverse students in school is elaborated in Cummins (1996). Here it is sufficient to note that literacy instruction can be viewed not only from a 'methods' perspective, but also from the perspective of the extent to which it fosters affirmation of students' identities and consequent motivation to engage academically. For example, there is little doubt that activating students' cognitive schemata represents an important instructional strategy for promoting text comprehension. However, in a classroom characterized by cultural and linguistic diversity, it also communicates strongly to students that what they know matters, that their voices will be heard in the classroom, and that their perspectives and cultural background can be shared with both the teacher and other students.

Similarly, instruction that is focused on helping students generate new knowledge (rather than just consuming information and skills), create literature and art, and act on social realities, is not only fostering higher-order cognitive and critical literacy skills, it is also creating an instructional context or space where students can demonstrate to their teachers and themselves what they are capable of achieving and who they are capable of becoming. In Vygotskian terms, the zone of proximal development is as much a zone of identity development as it is a zone of academic or cognitive development. This perspective infuses the three instructional foci that are sketched in the framework below. The framework attempts to integrate the research on reading and academic development among ELL students in such a way that its implications for classroom practice are evident.

An Instructional Framework

Within the framework sketched in Figure 1, *the Focus on Meaning* component argues that the interpretation of comprehensible input must go beyond mere literal comprehension and extend into critical literacy. Students should be encouraged to relate textual and instructional meanings to their own experience and prior knowledge (i.e. activate their cognitive schemata), critically analyze the information in the text (eg. evaluate the validity of various arguments or propositions) and use the results of their discussions and analyses in some concrete, intrinsically-motivating activity or project (eg. making a video or writing a poem or essay on a particular topic). This perspective is consistent with Fielding and Pearson's emphasis on the importance of providing students with frequent opportunities to discuss what they have read as a means of deepening comprehension.

In simple terms, the framework says that there must be engagement with meaning (messages) if students are to be motivated to participate. Students must see the relevance of the instruction to their lives. We know from the research that extensive reading is crucial for students' academic development. But what's the point of reading? If teachers cannot provide students with a convincing answer to this question then students are unlikely to read or develop academically.

Figure 1

INSTRUCTION FOR LANGUAGE LEARNING AND ACADEMIC ACHIEVEMENT

A.   FOCUS ON MEANING
Making Input Comprehensible
Developing Critical Literacy

B.   FOCUS ON LANGUAGE
Awareness of Language Forms and Uses
Critical Analysis of Language Forms and Uses

C.   FOCUS ON USE
Using Language to:
Generate New Knowledge
Create Literature and Art
Act on Social Realities

If students' background knowledge (their culture and language) is excluded from the teaching of reading and the interpretation of text, we will have violated one of the few principles that virtually all reading specialists agree on – the importance of activating students' cognitive schemata in the search for meaning.

The framework also says that we should provide students with explicit help in demystifying language and extend the range of contexts in which students can use language powerfully. Many of the silenced students in our classrooms are powerful users of language on the street. Once again, developing language awareness has got to be for a purpose, even if that purpose is simply to have fun with language. Thus, the teaching of phonics should be seen not as an isolated process but as part of the process of developing a critical awareness of language; in this way, it can be integrated into a powerful instructional focus that can extend through the grade levels. As outlined above, bringing students' knowledge of their L1 to bear on the interpretation of English text can be an extremely effective strategy. Lisa Delpit (1997) has argued along similar lines in the case of African-American students' knowledge of Ebonics and how it can support their acquisition of more standard forms of English.

More specifically, the *Focus on Language* component attempts to put controversial issues such as the appropriate time and ways to teach L2 grammar under the 'umbrella' of *Language Awareness*. The development of language awareness would include not just a focus on formal aspects of the language but also the following kinds of activities or projects focused on deepening students' knowledge of language and multilingual phenomena:

- The structure of language systems (eg. relationships between sounds and spelling, regional and class-based accents, grammar, vocabulary

- Ways of accomplishing different functions and purposes of language (eg. explaining, classifying, questioning, analyzing

- Conventions of different musical and literary forms (eg. rap, poetry, haiku, fiction, country music ballads

- Appropriateness of expression in different contexts (cultural conventions of politeness, street language versus school language, the language of everyday speech versus the language of books, language variety as a badge of identity in groups as diverse as gangs, political parties, fraternities

- Ways of organizing oral or written discourse to create powerful or persuasive messages (eg. oratorical speeches, influential written documents, political rhetoric, advertisements

- Diversity of language use in both monolingual and multilingual contexts (code-switching in bilingual communities, language maintenance and loss in families, political implications of the spread of English worldwide.

The *Focus on Use* component is based on the reality that L2 acquisition will remain abstract and largely trivial unless students have the opportunity to express themselves – their identities and their intelligence – through that language. There must be an authentic audience that motivates communication, ideally in both oral and written modes. In other words, the framework says that we can learn any language without using it.

From a linguistic point of view, attempting to use the language (in oral and written modes) shows us the gaps in our current knowledge and provides our teachers with the information they need to focus their instruction on helping us find the language we need to express ourselves effectively and powerfully.

More fundamentally, language use expresses to our peers, parents, teachers and to ourselves our insights, desires, hopes, histories, humour and concerns. It is a fundamental component in projecting ourselves from our past into the present and the future and becoming who we are. What motivates us to continue reading, writing and learning are these histories, insights, desires, hopes, humour and concerns – and if the interactions between teachers and students do not affirm the validity of this process then these interactions are not supporting learning.

Conclusion

Although this chapter has focused primarily on linguistic and cognitive issues in teaching ELL students, it is important to note that issues related to identity and power are equally important for understanding literacy and academic skills development. Particular instructional approaches must be assessed with respect to not only their effect on learning in a narrow sense but also their effectiveness in generating a sense of *empowerment*, understood as the collaborative creation of power between educators and students. Collaborative empowerment is essential to fostering long term academic engagement by means of affirming of students' identities and challenging the devaluation of students' cultural and linguistic identities in the wider society. Reading, writing, inquiry and learning are all intimately associated with the ways in which identities are being negotiated in the classroom. The development of sophisticated reading and writing skills can only occur in an instructional context where students are actively engaged in reading and writing. However, students will enthusiastically immerse themselves in these literacy activities only when both the process and products of these activities are affirming of their developing academic and personal identities.

Note

The recently published National Research Council (1998) report, *Preventing Reading Difficulties in Young Children* (chaired by Catherine Snow) articulated two broad conclusions with respect to teaching reading to ELL students:

> If language minority children arrive at school with no proficiency in English but speaking a language for which there are instructional guides, learning materials and locally available proficient teachers, then these children should be taught how to read in their native language while acquiring proficiency in spoken English, and then subsequently taught to extend their skills to reading in English.

> If language minority children arrive at school with no proficiency in English but speak a language for which the above conditions cannot be met and for which there are insufficient numbers of children to justify the development of the local community to meet such conditions, the instructional priority should be to develop the children's proficiency in spoken English. Although print materials may be used to develop understanding of English speech sounds, vocabulary, and syntax, the postponement of formal reading instruction is appropriate until an adequate level of proficiency in spoken English has been achieved.

Although these suggestions are reasonable, their emphasis is somewhat different than that which I have elaborated here. The focus on order of reading instruction (L1 before L2 where feasible) seems to me less significant than the extent to which there is a school-wide commitment to develop students' biliteracy skills and help them reap the cognitive benefits and metalinguistic insights associated with academic development in two or more languages.

Similarly, the report's emphasis on delaying English reading instruction until 'an adequate level of proficiency in spoken English' has been attained may underestimate the importance of providing a rich literacy environment in the early grades where children are literally surrounded by books and print and are listening to stories being read on a regular basis. The French immersion data (eg. Cashion and Eagan, 1990) suggest that in certain conditions reading can be taught through a second language even when students' fluency in that language is minimal.

Lefteris Doesn't Go To School Any Longer
From the Education of the Streets, to the Streets of Intercultural Education

Kostas Magos
The University of Athens, Greece

Lefteris was first registered at school when he was around ten years old. His name was Erol, a Turkish name, but he himself preferred the name Lefteris, a traditional Greek name, because it made him feel that he wasn't different from his classmates. He had never been to school before, and he hadn't attended nursery either. He was a Turkish-speaking Muslim, a child from the ethnic minority community, from a village in the mountains of Rodopi. He followed his parents who were working as cultivators in different regions of Greece, until they settled in Athens, when he was eight years old.

From age 8 to age 10, he didn't go to school but worked in the streets every day, selling tissues and cleaning windows. His father was unemployed and his mother worked as a cleaning lady. They had five children, three boys and two girls. The girls, none older than seventeen, were already married and had their own children. They were living all together in a small house behind a former gas factory, three kilometres from the centre of Athens.

When Lefteris first registered at school, he didn't know how to read and write either Greek or his home language. However, he did know how to speak and communicate in Greek. This was the unavoidable outcome of his rich social experience in the streets – that bore no similarity to the experiences of his classmates.

When the 10 year old Lefteris was registered at school, he was placed in the first grade. It was impossible for him to relate to the curriculum provided for the 6 year olds who were spelling 't'+'o'=to, 'm'+'e'=me and using completely age-inappropriate books for him. In an effort to make himself known and to overcome his boredom, he became naughty and even aggressive, ending up in the schoolmaster's office. He spent the breaks only with the Turkish-speaking children and his relationships with others was appalling. The others used words like 'gypsy' and 'gamin' when they spoke to him. So he became even more aggressive simply in an effort to defend himself, in an effort to exist.

As time passed, Lefteris started to stay away from school. At one stage he didn't turn up for weeks. We saw him in the streets around the school, sometimes on his own, sometimes with his brothers.

Then he reappeared. This time he refused to go into the first grade. He started trying different classrooms on his own, in an effort to find one where he could fit in. The courses didn't matter to him. He was not interested in them since he couldn't relate the classroom experiences to his everyday life; they had nothing to do with his problems and wanderings.

Unfortunately, little changed. After a few weeks in school, involved in frequent fights in the outdoor recreation area and in class, which drew threats and punishments, Lefteris began to be absent again, at first every now and then and then gradually building up to long absences from school. This went on for about three years, during which time, with the help of a few of his teachers, fewer of his classmates and with huge personal effort, he learned how to read and write in Greek.

For the whole period that Lefteris was coming to school, neither of his parents came to the school. But one of his older brothers regularly picked him up to do a 'job', as he called it. On one of these 'jobs', he was arrested. Lefteris had stolen a car. He came to school a couple of days later in a very bad state. Apart from the police violence, he had had to put up with the psychological pressure of his classmates and his parents, who had found out about what had happened. He stayed for a few more days and then he stopped attending for good. He didn't return. For Lefteris, education on the streets had won.

How many incidents of racism, how many acts of discrimination had left their mark on the face of young Lefteris, on the face of a child that happened to be a member of a group different from the majority?

First there was the racism of most of the educators, who have learned how to deal with only the children who follow the acceptable social norms. To these teachers, whether the individual is good or bad makes no difference; it's enough that those children deviate from the accepted models. Twenty five per cent of them believe unconditionally and 22% partly that Muslim students should be educated in separate schools – even though they are Greek citizens. Moreover, 73% of educators believe that the arrival of foreigners in Greece increases the incidence of crime, and 63% think that illegal immigrants should be sent back to their country.

Then there was the racism of the parents, who believed that their children would be in danger when a foreigner, a different student, appeared in the neighbourhood or class and whom they perceived as threatening the (falsely assumed) homogeneity of the class. In one of his school essays, entitled '*A Problem in Our Neighbourhood*', Fanis, one of Lefteris' classmates, wrote:

> '*Some foreigners come to our neighbourhood and hit us. A mum's child was beaten up so much that he had to go to hospital. That mum went around to all the mums in the neighbourhood and asked them to sign (...a petition) to make all foreigners leave the neighbourhood. All mums have signed and we will see what will happen.*

And then there was the racism of the children who, influenced by their parents and teachers, become the first crusaders to send away those who are different, those who disturb the outward appearance of balance of the school class. In a university study on the attitude of children in the Primary school towards 'the different', 63% of the children answered that they wouldn't like Rom children in their class and 56% said the same about Albanians. Nick, one of the children that took part in the study said, '*I don't want the Albanians because they steal. That's why I don't want them as my friends. Television says so as well.*'

The same study asked children the question: '*Which children from the following religions would you not like to sit with?*', and listed different religions. The highest rejection rate by the pupils was towards atheists (78%), followed by the Jehovah's Witnesses (72%) and Muslims (71%). Panagiotis, a pupil for whom 'Turk' and 'Muslim' are synonymous, said: '*The Turk's eye is always hovering over Greece. They have killed lots of people, we learn about it in history.*'

That is what Lefteris and all those like him face: the racism of a whole educational system and the society which preserves it. A society that doesn't care enough for the real and effective education of its members – because education is not just algebra and chemistry, not just learning by heart and being punished. It is far more to do with the interaction, communication, and the acceptance of and respect for difference.

The persistently ethnocentric educational system in Greece is interested in keeping the social balance always in favour of the majority, in order to school young people never to doubt the laws and their power. Everything different is dangerous, everything foreign is nightmarish. The school system serves the country's centralism. It is a special characteristic of the Greek system that it has abolished every effort of the different, of plurality and of non-conformity. The one and only analytic program, the single official textbook, the single educational source of study, keeps reinforcing the logic of homogeneity and uniformity and is addressed to a notional society that bears little resemblance to the diversity of the school population. This diversity does not just relate to children from different cultural groups but also to the range of differences ex-hibited by each child and every teacher in all schools – differences such as socio-economic origin, language and dialect, gender, sexuality, differing learning abilities, differing needs and different abilities and customs. All these are sacrificed on the altar of enforced 'common' values, ideologies and models that reproduce the dominant social norms.

Thousands are the victims of lesser or greater incidents of school racism, and the range of consequences is tragic – whether it is the murder of 12 year old Ahmed Iqbal Ullah by his white classmate at Burnage High School, England in 1986 or the student who withdraws from studies and abandons school because s/he can no longer stand being mocked, ridiculed, insulted and threatened.

But there are also all those who put up with the racism and, little by little, bury their real selves in an effort to hide their difference and try to be like the others. Take Fatme from Iran, who prefers to be called Fotini. She is a twelve year old student in fifth grade in Athens who, although Muslim, crosses her heart in the morning prayer – maybe she goes to Sunday school, who knows – dyes her black hair blonde, and declares that her grandfather is Greek.

So what should be changed in the educational system so as to make Fatme accept her real identity and not send Lefteris-Erol back to the streets? What will help each child to develop without ruining the special and different parts of their personality and identity? The only educational way is surely intercultural education.

Intercultural education prepares people for a multicultural society where differences will be freely expressed and can be equally accepted. It is education that respects difference from wherever it may come and cultivates the dual principal of unity in difference and difference in unity. Intercultural education is not a written study of different cultures: it openly fights against all kinds of racism and discrimination; it battles social division and xenophobia; it gives a hand to everyone – not just the nationally different but also those who are different within the same national group. It supports equal chances and rights for everybody and can lead to social change.

Recent multicultural education programs in the US, Canada, Australia, Europe and Greece all indicate that no educational reformation is possible without the participation of the people involved. Only where the educational changes occurred alongside the community and not in isolation were results positive. Where the school opened its doors, where teachers, parents and students commonly decided the how and why of education, shared the curriculum, chose the books and the ways of working, education was fruitful. Intercultural education reached its goals where schools were no longer isolated from life but reformed into a living and creative social centres.

Such schools are proof that intercultural education can be realised. They are the seeds for deeper educational and social change. In Greece the reality is that such education is only beginning. There had been no anticipation in the public education system of the needs of children with different cultural identity, children of refugees or immigrants. If they had the right documentation, which they usually didn't, they could be registered at school and be taught the same courses from the same books and in the same way as Greek-speaking children. Reception or support classes were there to provide some help. But most of these students, although regularly attending school for many years, remained functionally illiterate. The efforts of a few educators to stand by them were undermined by the difficult conditions under which they worked – large numbers of students in every class, poor substructure, shortage of appropriate books and pedagogic material. This is still the general picture, but lately there is a glimmer of light. Efforts are apparent in many schools, sometimes at the unique initiative of certain educators, sometimes with the co-operation of the university or other outside agencies. Interesting initiatives are emerging, such as the pilot program in one Athenian primary school with around 60% of children from ethnic minorities, supported the Department of Pre-school Education of Athens University.

The goal of the program is full communication and equal access for these children to the learning provided in the school. Experiential learning, in-service training for teachers, production of multi-cultural materials and co-operation with other schools are being introduced. Recently a series of afternoon workshops were held on creativity and communication – currently only for children but later to be extended to parents. It is a pioneering program for Greece and has had to overcome initial problems, be self-supporting and self maintaining. It is put to the test every day.

Educational programs that target access to education for different cultural identities are being conducted for Muslims, people from the former Soviet Union and Rom in many regions of the country. These programs are still in the early stages so cannot yet be evaluated, but their existence shows an important shift in intention and an effort to change the Greek educational system; efforts encouraged by increasing calls from more and more groups for another kind of education. Students, youngsters, educators and parents who refuse the traditional, anachronistic and inhumane model of education are envisioning a different and diverse society woven round schools, neighbourhood centres and clubs and cultural movements, supported by educational and other material and resources. They gather together and talk, protest, propose, declare and stir up the 'stagnant lake' of Greek education.

The banner of these groups, on view at students' demonstrations but also at strikes, is 'Education For All'. The call is out for education that is open to everyone, respects differences and that is directed against discrimination. To make this dream come true is in our hands.

Notes

- Rodopi is a region in Northern Greece, close to Turkey. Part of its population belongs to what is called the Muslim minority, in contrast with the majority of Greeks who are Christians. Most have Turkish as their home language.
- In the Greek educational system there is only one official school textbook for each course and educators are obliged to follow it.

The Power of Babel: Collaboration and Empowerment – (an extract)

Viv Edwards

Reading and Language Information Centre,
The University of Reading, UK

The Reading and Language Information Centre at the University of Reading has frequently benefited in recent years from the opportunities for networking and co-operation offered by the Intercultural Education Partnership. Much of our own research is informed by the same philosophy as that of the partnership. In particular, some of our recent work with teachers and children points to two principles – collaboration and empowerment – which, we believe, are critical to an understanding of how schools and classrooms develop and change. The initiatives in question all focused in different ways on culturally and linguistically diverse classrooms.

(The following is an extract from the report, 'The Power of Babel: Collaboration and Empowerment' – 1999, into several of the Centre's recent projects, listed at the end of the extract. It focuses on the involvement of bilingual parents in a multilingual word processing project.)

The Multilingual Word Processing in the Primary School project

As we surveyed multilingual classroom resources, we realised that the most important producers of multilingual resources were not commercial publishers but children, teachers and parents. This led us logically to a research initiative: the Multilingual Word Processing in the Primary School Project – a multidisciplinary effort involving linguists, teachers and designers at the University of

Reading and planned in close co-operation with the headteacher and staff at the case study school – Redlands Primary School in Reading. We wanted to chart the issues involved in introducing word processing in a non-Latin script into a primary school. The language in question in this instance was Urdu using the program Page Composer.

Our starting point was the teachers and children and what they wanted to happen. Because of the shortage of suitable materials in their languages, they wanted to use the software to produce a wider range of resources – both single language materials in Urdu and dual language texts in Urdu and English – and they envisaged that these would be produced by various collaborations by teachers, parents and children. They were also excited at the possibilities the software offered for communication with parents, including letters home and Urdu versions of school documents such as the Governors' Report (which had previously been handwritten). They felt it was important, too, that parents should be able to use the new program. There was a general consensus that the software would allow children to develop and apply their ICT capability, make good use of their bilingual skills and support their literacy development in Urdu.

• Introducing the package

At the outset a great deal of time was spent discussing the best ways of introducing the software to pupils and parents. The most obvious route was through the weekly lunchtime Urdu club, but staff were anxious to find ways of informing the wider school community, including Pakistani parents, of what was taking place.

Early concern about reactions to the program proved completely unfounded. Women who had previously been reluctant to have anything to do with computers were clearly interested and excited at seeing the word 'Welcome' written in Urdu on the screen, and half a dozen attended a workshop where they helped produce stories in Urdu for their children. They worked very much as a community of writers, being guided by an Urdu speaking teacher but also supporting each other.

Following this initial workshop, parents voiced their interest in coming in to school on a regular basis to practice their word processing skills. A form of cascade training gradually evolved, with a member of staff working with one particularly enthusiastic mother and she, in turn, helping other parents and children.

• *Looking back*

As we reflected on the events of eighteen months following the introduction of the software, it was clear that the outputs of multilingual word processing anticipated at the outset of the project had been achieved. However, other benefits were possibly more noteworthy. Perhaps the most notable achievement of the project was the greater level of parental involvement which it had achieved, allowing a number of women whose English was limited and who had previously felt unable to take part in school-related activities to make a contribution to their children's school learning for the first time.

The high public profile sent powerful messages to all the parents and children in the school about the importance which it attaches to linguistic diversity. There were also benefits for individual Pakistani parents: the school was able to offer a training opportunity and word processing facilities for personal and community use. Teachers also benefited. They were able to take stock of their current use of both multilingual resources and computers in the classroom. The project helped to highlight ICT training needs and associated classroom management issues. It also challenged some commonly held assumptions about bilingual parents and showed that the level of parental involvement in school can be significantly raised.

The impact of Urdu wordprocessing on the children was dramatic. Regular attendance at the weekly Urdu club grew and non-Urdu speakers also joined. Within a relatively short time, a third of children attending were from English families, suggesting that the status associated with new technologies has been transferred to Urdu in the eyes of both Urdu and English speakers. Pakistani children acquired far greater confidence both in the use of computers and in the development of writing skills in Urdu. They were also enjoying their newly acquired expert status.

• *Empowerment*

The theme which emerged from this project (*and the other research projects in its report*) is one of empowerment. The Multilingual Word processing in the Primary School Project witnessed the active participation of parents who had previously not played a part in their children's formal schooling learning, in producing learning materials and helping children use the Urdu software. Some mothers also took advantage of the opportunity to develop word processing skills for their own use out of school. Pakistani children, for their part, were empowered to act as peer tutors for word processing in Urdu, and as language learning models for their English speaking peers.

Projects

Multilingual Resources for Children Project (MRC, 1995; Edwards and Walker, 1996; Edwards and Walker, in press)

Multilingual Wordprocessing in the Primary School Project (Chana *et al*, 1997; 1998);

GEST 16 Meeting the Needs of Bilingual Pupils Project (called the Teacher Training project in this publication) (Edwards, 1998)

Fabula: Bilingual Multimedia Educational Materials for children.
www.fabula.eu.org

Further information on these projects is available at: www.ralic.reading.ac.uk

'Mum, Let's Learn Together!'
some examples of parental participation using the mother tongue

Joke Kypriotakis

Beatrixschool, Rotterdam, The Netherlands

Beatrix Primary School is situated in a suburb of Rotterdam. Our school has a population of about 300 pupils, of whom 65% are immigrant children from 25 different nationalities. Primary school pupils are between 4 and 12 years old, so we do not have a separate kindergarten.

My school is facing a sudden change of population, as many immigrants prefer to move from the older parts of the city to the suburbs. I remember when in the seventies we had our first black pupil from Surinam; at the beginning of the eighties two Turkish boys entered the school, and currently only one in six new entrants is Dutch. Most of the immigrant children at the moment come from our former colonies, the Antilles and Surinam. We also host refugee children from former Yugoslavia, Russia, Iran and African countries like Somalia and Zaire.

Rotterdam has about 600,000 inhabitants, most of them finding jobs in all kinds of industries related to the harbour – the largest in the world. Some neighbourhoods have very old, cheap houses, and that is where a concentration of immigrant families can be found. There are about 30,000 children aged 4 or under in the city. 73% of them are children of immigrants or have parents with low level of jobs (or no job) and poor education. As an important harbour city, Rotterdam has a long history of hosting people from all over the world. The development of educational programmes for migrant children dates from the late sixties.

In 1993 the Ministry of Education made a four-year agreement with the city of Rotterdam for educational innovations with the following aims:

- Promoting pre-school activities. In 1993 only 19% of the 0-4 year old children went to a creche. More creches were founded with special attention for immigrant parents, who seldom sent their children to creches. This means that most of their children have little contact with the Dutch language till the age of 4, when they go to school.

- Improving the quality of the pre-school activities, including the training of creche 'teachers'. Many training programs were established and the standard of activities offered improved considerably.

- Integrating and adopting creche and primary-school activities. Teachers from both sectors exchanged ideas and educational experiences, paying special attention to learning Dutch as a second language.

- Paying special attention to Dutch as a second language. This resulted in the Rotterdam DELTA plan project, where primary schools analyse their language teaching and, with the support of the Educational Service Centre, develop their own policy, with additional provision for children whose mother tongue is not Dutch. Evaluation of the project showed that it had produced spectacular results.

- The last and most important aim was encouraging parental participation. The vision is that the support of the parents enhances the efficiency of teaching. All kinds of small projects started, informing parents about the educational system in Holland, about shared control, parents' councils, obligations and responsibilities concerning their children's education. Parents were offered the possibility to be partners in developing educational aims.

We asked ourselves the following questions:

- How can we reach, inform and instruct parents, as they themselves cannot understand the language we are speaking?

- How can we reach parents if they rarely enter the school?

- How can we involve them in education, if they consider the school as a 'high authority' institution?

- How can we exploit the parents' expertise in their mother tongues?

- What exactly is our vision on parental participation?

- Do we consider parents as consumers or as concerned parties with responsibilities in the parental council or the school-board, or as volunteers, giving all kinds of practical help, or – most importantly – as educational partners?

This latter vision is what my school is committed to. Children learn far better at school when they have the assistance and interest of their parents at home.

Our school faced a gigantic problem with pupils who had limited vocabulary even in their mother tongue. So for us it was of great importance that the children also developed a rich vocabulary in the mother tongue. And it would be a mistake to think that only the immigrant children have poor vocabularies. In this society with TV and video inhibiting interaction between people, some Dutch minors also lack vocabulary skills. We had to run this blockade by exploring the mother tongue and the parental assistance in the home situation. A further challenge was to break through the isolation of many of the immigrant mothers.

That is when the idea of using para-professionals who speak the mother tongues was born. We developed our vision with the following aims:

- Promoting parental education-supporting behaviour. This behaviour would include taking an active interest in the school system and in the progress and activities of their children, and maintaining good contacts with the school.

- Encouraging the school to give parents opportunities for participating, not sit back waiting for the parents to take the initiative. Schools have to provide parents with the tools for participation.

- Promoting contacts between parents of different nationalities. Immigrant mothers can be rather isolated and facing stress and loneliness. It is vital that a social network is created among the pupils' mothers. If mothers are feeling positive their children will benefit. Besides, with the great danger of increasing racism and fascism, it is valuable for people to know each other better and learn to respect their different cultural backgrounds.

- Ensuring that the school relate to home activities to the contents of school activities. There is pedagogical advantage when the school and the home situation are in a kind of balance. Co-operation between teacher and parent affects the child, enhancing the parents' affection for the child and the teachers' professional love.

- Promoting the learning of Dutch as a second language. We believe that it is important that children know the meaning of words in their mother tongue. To translate them later into another language will then be easier. We also found that many speakers of Dutch as a first language had a restricted vocabulary in their mother tongue.

- Promoting positive interaction between mother and child. Usually when I talk of parental participation, I am referring to mothers because in practice it is mostly they who are in contact with the school, but I do not exclude the fathers, and indeed met fathers who participated – but they were in the minority. I also met grandparents, when both parents worked. In many societies, raising a child is a family matter, where neighbours, grandparents, aunts and uncles also feel responsible for the well-being of the child. Many immigrant mothers miss the support and involvement of their relatives while raising their children. They miss the advice and the shared responsibility, and they do not know how to bear the heavy task of being an educator.

Also in Dutch society (and I suppose in every modern European country) parents have or take less time to pursue activities with their children. We are living in the age of TV, video, computer games and violence, with much less human contact than even 25 years ago. Accordingly, the Rotterdam Seagull Foundation, which was appointed to develop the program, defined five conditions for methodology.

The method should be:

- flexible, connected to the situation in the school. The starting point is not related to any particular subject or time during the school year

- available as much as possible in the mother-tongue. There are Turkish and Moroccan versions of the program. Thus, parents are stimulated to use their own language, so that at least the children know the notions in their own language

- attractive and inviting. The method requires about fifteen minutes of attention a day, so is not onerous

- inviting of exploration, which takes place mostly at school in a group of parents. It is important to build a social network, to exchange ideas and hear about the experiences of others. Parents support and stimulate each other. They are asked to come to school once a week or fortnightly for just half an hour of instruction.

In addition, the program must support parents so that they feel more confident about their own abilities to guide their children. Relationships between parents and children are likely to improve; as children talk about what they are doing, the parents support this in the mother-tongue and at the same time learn some words in Dutch from the children.

Three people in our school were essential to the running of the program: our bilingual para-professionals.

Horia is a 19 year-old Moroccan and speaks Arabic and Dutch. Until ten months ago her life was a mess: she quit school, did not know what to do, and lived on social welfare. Through a special community project in Rotterdam to encourage young immigrants to make something of their lives, she was directed to me, to see if she would like a job as an educational assistant. She turned out to have a natural talent for working with young children. For the first time we could communicate with the Moroccan mothers – who soon trusted her and us. Horia did and does an excellent job, especially with the 4 year old Moroccan children who enter the school with no knowledge of Dutch, where she becomes an intermediary. She is now enrolled at a professional institute, studying children's education. This young immigrant now knows what her aim in life is.

Bildan is Turkish. After being regularly beaten up by her husband, she decided to take their child and run away – for which her family has rejected her. She was living on social welfare, but under the new national policy she is obliged to find a job. To keep her entitlement to social welfare she works with us helping the Turkish children and parents. As she had no education for such a job, I tutor her. She has also started training to become an assistant for parental participation.

Fadima is Moroccan. She speaks Berber and Arabic. As a 10 year old girl who had never been to school, she was brought by her father to the Netherlands. She had to help her mother bring up her younger brothers and sisters. She did not attend school in the Netherlands and when she was 16 her father found her a husband. She divorced, is no longer accepted in her own family, and takes care of her life and the life of her two children. She learned to read and write Dutch on her own, and is very motivated to work to qualify for social welfare. Like Bildan, she is studying to become an assistant for parental participation. They attend the course for one day a week.

The Dutch parents had to get used to these three immigrant helpers working mainly in the first and second years of the school, but now they are well accepted and appreciated. The school is responsible for these helpers; they have special tasks and do not work on their own initiative, but inform the management about what they do. Each week they organise meetings with the parents, in Turkish, Berber, Arabic and also Dutch. They give out the material and instruction for games and tasks that all parents are expected to do with their children. Matters such as going to the library, the community centre, the doctor, hospital, healthy food, and courses for parents can also be discussed in the meetings over a cup of tea or coffee. If needed, help is provided with filling in forms. Para-professionals are taught to work with staff to organise educational meetings with parents about such issues as discipline, choosing toys, obedience and encouragement.

In several Rotterdam schools, almost 98% of the parents join a special project called the RUGZAK project. For six weeks an assistant in parental participation takes materials to the family and gives instruction to the parents, for example about how to play hide and seek or 'guess what I am saying'. She also provides parents with picture books and stories in their mother tongue. For illiterate parents the instructions are available in pictorial form. After the first six weeks the parents meet in a group in the community centre. The program has about sixty different activities and familiarises parents with different games, institutions like the public library, toy rental organisations and so on.

The RUGZAK project is used for the first two years in primary school and is available in Turkish, Arabic and Dutch. The children are given a rucksack containing colouring pencils, glue, a pair of scissors, a pencil sharpener, a picture book and an eraser. Instruction is given by the education assistants in the mother tongue. The Dutch parents also participate. Parents thus become involved in the educational progress of their children.

While parents become accustomed to their role as partners in education, a second project – OVERSTAP – continues to oversee their activities with the children. OVERSTAP is a literacy project, helping parents to support their children's reading development. It is available in six languages: Arabic, Turkish, English, Portuguese, Spanish and Dutch. Spread over the year, there are ten instructional meetings of parents and the teacher of Dutch in the school every three or four weeks. The para-professional assists only in the case where the parents do not understand Dutch.

OVERSTAP uses a shared-reading book with ten different stories in the six languages. There are ten different reading books, two audio cassettes with those stories on it, and ten activity books. The activities take the parents about ten minutes a day, and shows them step by step how their child discovers the magic of learning to read. At the time of writing 100% of the parents were participating.

After some years of working with para-professionals, we have found that the positive results for the children are considerable:

- the children like doing the games
- they feel an important member in the family
- children with no toys of their own have the opportunity to borrow and use a range of toys
- children learn and talk together
- their vocabulary and pronunciation improves significantly.

and for the parents:

- interaction between parent and child is improved
- parents become used to listening to their child and showing interest
- they learn how to ask questions
- they start inventing activities on their own
- they talk with other parents about education
- they feel more attached to the school

- many parents increase their Dutch vocabulary by doing the activities with their child

- they break out of their isolation.

There are positive results also for the school, too, in the form of:

- better contact with parents

- better academic results, especially in verbal language teaching.

There are positive results for the bilingual paraprofessionals who now have challenging and rewarding occupations. And finally, working with the para-professionals is enriching pupils, parents, school and the whole community.

Success ultimately depends on the quality of the para-professionals and the school's enthusiasm and support. It is worth considering whether such an approach can be equally enriching and rewarding in other countries.

Teaching Academic Language to Pupils with EAL

Carrie Cable

We are all aware of pupils we have taught who have rapidly learnt the social language of the classroom and playground (BICS – Basic Interpersonal Communication Skills) but who have then reached a plateau in terms of their learning. Often these pupils have learnt to read and write narrative forms with considerable success but have difficulty with 'imaginative' writing and the demands of the wider curriculum in terms of non-narrative, non-chronological reading and writing in different genres (CALP – Cognitive Academic Language Proficiency) (Cummins, 1992).

A number of different reasons for this can be suggested:

- the discontinuing of specific EAL support by specialist teachers after basic fluency has been achieved

- the establishment of a dependency culture in the pupils and an unwillingness on their part to take risks

- overuse of linguistically and cognitively undemanding tasks in order to keep pupils occupied

- the knowledge, skills and understanding acquired in the first language (L1) compartmentalised away from the second language (L2) and the opportunities for pupils to make links between their previous and new language experiences limited

- little or no explicit planning to meet the language development needs of bilingual pupils

- opportunities for learners to make connections between new and existing knowledge restricted

- opportunities for pupils to make connections between speech and writing restricted

- inadequate explicit teaching of the difference between narrative and non-narrative texts

- inadequate explicit teaching of different non-narrative forms in reading and writing

- limited opportunities for learners to hear language modelled by teachers and fluent English speaking peers

- opportunities for pupils to practice new forms and registers in a supportive environment restricted

- little or no teacher scaffolding to support learning

- lack of corrective feedback.

This is not an exhaustive list and readers will be able to add their own suggestions. But for the purposes of discussion, I would like to focus on some of these areas and suggest some possible strategies to support pupils' continuing language development.

Making connections between first and second language knowledge and experience

There is extensive research (eg. Collier and Thomas and 1995) to suggest that pupils are more successful in acquiring English and developing academic language if they are in bilingual programmes. Yet still in the UK pupils are rarely enabled to use their knowledge and skills in the L1 in learning L2. Our system, at best, allows for the use of L1 in the first few years at school in order to provide a transition to English, after which it is generally ignored until GCSE level, when some schools make provision for students to take, or in rare cases study, their community language for GCSE. What happens in between is left to parents and community classes.

In her chapter on 'Policy and Practice in Bilingual Education', Hornberger (1995) stresses the importance of 'connect and transfer' in helping pupils to make explicit connections across two languages. One of the teachers in her research study activity encourages the use of translation by pupils, encourages them to analyse the features of language and discuss and reason about how texts are constructed and what the essential differences are between different types of texts.

We know that attitudes towards the use of home languages by bilingual pupils have changed in the last thirty years. Many teachers recognise that pupils do have language experience in languages other than English and try, through displays for example, to acknowledge the languages spoken in a school. However, few attempts are made to enable pupils to actively use their L1 skills and experiences to connect and transfer their knowledge of reading, writing, text construction and purpose. A language support teacher may provide or encourage pupils to develop word banks with L1 translations but this work is usually done purely at an individual level and the results rarely become part of the resources for a subject. Opportunities for pupils to connect and transfer their knowledge, skills and understanding also rarely operate beyond the vocabulary level and pupils are rarely provided with opportunities to apply this strategy at the sentence or discourse level.

Yet we all know that learning to read involves more than learning to read words. Fluent readers draw on a wide range of knowledge, skills and understanding to draw meaning from texts. As well as their linguistic and grammatical knowledge, readers draw on their knowledge of how different texts are organised, structured and presented as narratives or to convey information for different purposes. They draw on a range of skills in order to process information and make decisions about relevance and the purposes of reading. They also draw on their social and cultural experience of texts and reading, on how they may have been taught to read at home or in community language classes and their literacy experiences outside school. So why is so little attention focused on these crucial aspects of reading for bilingual pupils?

Most teachers teach from within their own cultural traditions and, especially if they are monolingual themselves or have received not specific training, they may have difficulty in appreciating the range of knowledge their bilingual pupils have to draw on or the importance of enabling pupils to make connections. However, if teachers believe that building on and activating pupils' prior knowledge is a crucial part of learning, then it should not be impossible for them to see that knowledge of their L1 and the knowledge, skills and understanding gained through it needs to be recognised and activated to allow the pupils to progress both linguistically and cognitively.

The research by Thomas and Collier (1995) clearly indicates that bilingual pupils or pupils with ESL/EAL who have been educated in programmes which have included dual language teaching of the curriculum or a substantial amount of bilingual education coupled with L2 taught through academic content will perform substantially better than their monolingual peers or ESL/EAL pupils who do not receive a substantial amount of their education through bilingual programmes or second language teaching taught through academic content. Interestingly, their research indicates that pupil progress in the first three years of their schooling (grades 1-3 in the USA) is similar irrespective of the type of programme that pupils are involved in; the effects of the type of programmes pupils have been involved in become noticeable as the pupils progress through the educational system.

What can we do in the British context? Bilingual teachers are better able to provide teaching in and through L1 than monolingual teachers and we should continue to press for adequately funded and resourced provision to ensure that this is possible in the future. However, there are possibilities for monolingual teachers too. The following is an example of a unit of work developed by an EAL teacher and a class teacher attempts to draw on some of the principles discussed above.

The aim of this unit of work was to develop pupils' understanding of the specificity of language through work about strawberries. Pupils were given opportunities to focus on exploring descriptive language and to examine, compare and contrast a range of text types and develop a range of writing around this theme. The following elements were taken into account in planning this work:

- careful planning for oral work

- activating pupils' prior knowledge of story, song, poem, rhyme

- providing concrete examples

- providing visual support and stimuli

- planning to ensure bilingual pupils would have expertise to contribute

- planning activities to scaffold pupils' learning

- planning for different learning outcomes

- planning for peer group support and teacher modelling

- organising groupings to maximise learning for all pupils

- making the learning outcomes explicit to the pupils.

In groups, pupils had to focus on a strawberry and build up descriptive words and phrases in as many different languages as possible moving from words describing colour, shape and size, to words describing smell, texture and taste. The pupils developed their own concept maps to use as the basis for future work. The word 'nice' was banned. Pupils then developed similes and compared and contrasted these in different languages. They noted their points in their groups, exchanged ideas (and other language information) and went on to write about strawberries in a variety of genres. Beforehand the teachers read different texts to the pupils, i.e. narrative, poetry, plays, recipes, descriptions, reports and the pupils compared the different kinds of writing, making explicit how they differed in terms of organisation, presentation, style, word choice, ease or reading, purpose etc. The pupils had to focus carefully on language forms and structures, make decisions about appropriacy and suitability, and use their knowledge and understanding of language in a structured but imaginative way and made contributions in other languages an important element in completing tasks. Ultimately the pupils presented their writing to the rest of the class and made displays for the classroom.

Developing the four language skills simultaneously and making connections between speech and writing

My second concern is that pupils need to develop the four language skills simultaneously and teachers need to enable them to see the similarities and differences between these skills.

We know that some language learners go through a 'silent period', when they do not appear to participate but are listening and making connections – given the right environment and appropriate teaching. For some time research tended to focus on how similar learning a second language is to learning the first. But there have always been those who challenged this suggestion and pointed out that when children are learning their first language, they have opportunities to listen and make connections in stress-free conditions and have plenty of time to play with words and experiment with talk before they begin to read and write. Many pupils learning EAL are, as we know, faced with the challenge of acquiring all the systems at the same time while not being consciously encouraged or allowed to use the systems they have already acquired in their first language. Pupils are having to acquire processing skills, listening and reading at the same time as production skills, speaking and writing. And they are also having to disentangle two different systems – of the spoken and of the written word.

Pupils need to learn the differences between the spoken and written word in order to develop the range of registers and genres required for academic achievement. Many writers have highlighted the differences between spoken and written texts in terms of vocabulary, sentence and discourse organisation and the fact that the differences are greatest between speech and non-fiction texts (see, amongst others Perera, 1984). We know that opportunity for talk varies in classrooms according to the skills and planning of the teachers but we also know that much of the early talk pupils with EAL engage in is 'conversational' and involves commands, questions, exclamations and non-statement sentences and that there is often much repetition. The amount and kinds of talk in the classroom are, however, all too often restricted and do little to develop pupils' oral skills beyond the social or to provide pupils with opportunities to become reflective thinkers and learners. As teachers, we need to make more explicit the connections and differences between the spoken and written word and create opportunities for pupils to move backwards and for-wards between the two forms.

Most bilingual pupils are taught a range of strategies to help them with learning to read, although phonic knowledge has been em-phasised in the National Literacy Strategy. One issue that teachers constantly raise is that pupils seem to be unable to understand what they have read, particularly when it is non-fiction. As part of their assessment and monitoring procedures, many teachers have examined pupils' comprehension skills, compared them with their fluency as readers – and found that their fluency was disguising a lack of understanding. We all know of pupils who can decode or *decipher* (Meek, 1988) texts but can recall or explain little when questioned. This seems to apply particularly to unfamiliar narrative and non-fiction texts. The action research project being carried out by Frederickson and colleagues of University College London looked at the reading behaviour and performance on a range of tests of 50 Bengali/Sylheti pupils in Tower Hamlets. Their initial con-clusions would suggest that these bilingual pupils perform as well as their monolingual peers in terms of grapho-phonic knowledge but significantly less well in terms of reading comprehension (Frederickson, 1997). Other research studies in progress appear to be drawing similar conclusions (eg. Cline, 1998).

Difficulties in comprehension tend to become more obvious as pupils enter Key Stage 2 and 3 and come into contact with more non-fiction texts. This is when the gap between fluency and range of experience widens for bilingual pupils. Non-fiction texts differ from fiction in terms of lexis, sentence and discourse organisation as well as in terms of density of information. Also, there are many different kinds of non-fiction text types. But bilingual pupils are either not exposed to non-fiction texts when they are being taught to read or they are not taught to read the text in a meaningful way. The reading strategies taught are not the skills that will help pupils to extract meaning from texts because of over-emphasis on the teaching of grapho-phonic knowledge at the expense of explicit teaching of the semantic and syntactic systems so crucial for making meaning from texts.

The syntactic and semantic cueing systems rely on pupils' ability to predict what meanings are by drawing on the topic in general, their familiarity with similar texts, their knowledge of grammatical or structure words and their cultural knowledge about text types and text conventions. What pupils know about the context of the text, the preparation they do before reading it, the opportunities to discuss it, the visual support, the opportunities to make connections with their prior knowledge or with knowledge they have in L1, and the teacher's knowledge of the pupils starting points are all crucial factors in how pupils in access the semantic cueing system.

Access to the syntactic system requires that pupils understand about word order, about how verbs change according to tense, how words endings change, how auxiliary verbs change the meaning of verbs, how connectives and conjunctions link ideas, how different articles are used for different purposes, and how pronouns can change meanings.

Pupils will be able to make meaning of texts if teachers develop pupils' semantic and syntactic knowledge bases as well as their lexical knowledge base. Fluency in reading can disguise lack of understanding which, if it is allowed to continue, will make pupils either reluctant to acknowledge that they do not understand or develop strategies to carry out tasks to please teachers or their peers. The closed question: 'Do you understand?' will often elicit the reply: 'Yes', whether or not the pupil has actually understood. More open questions that probe understanding will often reveal misunderstandings or lack of comprehension. The knowledge gained from questioning of this kind can help teachers to plan ways for pupils to acquire the language experiences they need. We also need to teach pupils strategies to help them signal whether or not they have understood a text, and how to analyse and compare and contrast different text types.

Bilingual pupils in our schools find themselves having to develop the four language skills virtually simultaneously in English in order to achieve academically. Pupils have to learn to listen, speak, read and write English all at the same time to access the content of the curriculum and the enormous amount of new information they are bombarded with. So teachers need to devise opportunities for them to do this and one way is to help pupils to make links between the spoken and written word.

Most teachers are now familiar with DARTs activities (Directed Activities Related to Texts) and the two types of activities – analysis and reconstruction. Some DARTs activities can effectively help pupils to make explicit the links between reading, writing and speech through a variety of planned activities.

Both teachers and pupils generally expect there to be a written outcome to any task and there is enormous pressure on teachers to provide 'evidence' of pupils' learning. But it is important also to provide opportunities for pupils to focus on texts and plan for oral outcomes. For example a matching activity with teacher-prepared texts which illustrate photographs or diagrams can provide opportunities for pupils to focus on the structure of the prepared texts. This can be preceded by pupil discussion about the photographs or diagrams (without the prepared text) and pupil-generated descriptions of the photographs or explanations of the diagrams, which can be compared with the teacher generated versions. The texts used to illustrate different subject matter can be analysed by pupils and compared and contrasted to highlight different text types, text structures and purposes.

Reporting back to the class on the outcome of a practical task or investigation allows pupils to focus closely on the language they will need to describe what they have done and what they have found out. This oral work can also provide an important scaffolding stage in writing, as Pauline Gibbons (1991) illustrates.

> The first extract is a spoken text produced by a group of children involved in a Science lesson.
>
> *try this one ... no it doesn't go ... it doesn't matter ... try that ... yes ... it does a bit ... it won't work ... it's not metal ... these are the best ... it's making them go really fast.*
>
> The second text is what the children reported back to the rest of the class
>
> *We tried a pin, a pencil sharpener, some iron filings and a piece of plastic. The magnet didn't attract the pin, but it did attract the pencil sharpener and the iron filings, It didn't attract the plastic.*
>
> The third text is an example of one child's writing about the experiment
>
> *Our experiment was to find out what a magnet attracted. We discovered that a magnet attracts some kinds of metal. It attracted the iron filings, but not the pin. It also did not attract things that were not metal.*
>
> (Gibbons, 1991 pp.30–31

When bilingual pupils first begin to write they often write dialogue, especially if they have been reluctant to begin writing until they feel more confident about spoken English. They opt for the speech forms with which they are familiar in their writing. A way to capitalise on this process is to build in opportunities for conversation or dialogue writing as a DARTs type reconstruction activity.

Pupils can be involved in constructing conversations from information texts, or vice versa, and then compare their texts with those of other pupils. The following example is adapted from Gillham (1986).

Information Text

Asteroids are lumps of rock and metal whose paths round the sun lie mainly between Mars and Jupiter. Asteroids are really small planets though some are no bigger than houses and the largest is only 480 miles wide. Only one of the asteroids, Vesta, can occasionally be seen by the naked eye in the night sky.

Conversation Text

Ameena	What are asteroids, Patrick?
Patrick	They are lumps of rock and metal that move around the sun. Most of them follow orbits between the planets Mars and Jupiter. Asteroids are planets, really, but they are not usually called planets because they are so small.
Ameena	How big are they then?
Patrick	Well the smallest ones are only about the size of a house. The biggest is 480 miles wide.
Ameena	Could I see any of them in the sky at night?
Patrick	There is only one you could see without a telescope. It's called Vesta but you wouldn't be able to see it very often.

It is important to make explicit the differences between the text types and activities of this kind provide opportunities to do so. Comparisons between texts can also be used to teach aspects of the syntactic and semantic cueing systems and to examine textual cohesion (eg the pronoun referents in this text). Reconstruction activities are also good checks on comprehension. Teachers need to plan to give pupils opportunities to derive meaning from whole texts, even brief ones, and not just from sentences and words. Giving pupils opportunities to activate their prior knowledge means for bilingual pupils that they have to make links with the knowledge and understanding they have gained and are still gaining of and in L1 and their developing knowledge and understanding in L2. Pupils need to be able to make connections and to transfer this knowledge and understanding so that they become confident and successful learners.

A Holistic Approach to Second Language Assessment and Planning
using and developing the full repertoire

Tim Parke

University of Hertfordshire, UK

Language as Difference

This chapter sets out the wide range of conditions under which children with English as an additional language are expected to acquire English and to relate these conditions to current second language acquisition. It examines three texts from such children and evaluates their strengths and weaknesses, both linguistic and pragmatic/functional and what this suggests about the range of support for children learning English as an additional language. It is useful to begin by looking briefly at the role language serves for children who experience more than one in their early years, just when they become aware of linguistic variation.

Trying to look at language 'from the inside', as a user might see it, is inherently paradoxical, because much language use and perhaps nearly all early language use is unconscious. In many cases, language is just a tool for certain purposes, which we use to interact with others, to attain certain things, and sometimes for play. It is a truism that language is learned but not taught, and that explicit correction is valueless. In fact parents do seem to value certain norms in speech – accent is a prominent factor for some parents, taboo or vulgar words another. But overall the acquisition process is largely unconscious. Children become members of a speech community in the same way that they become members of the community in general, and they acquire expectations about how language is used, for instance, about turn-taking in conversations and the difference between child/adult and child/child conversations. Language development, the move towards native-speaker competence, proceeds with little intervention and therefore with only minor acknowledgement of progress. Parents and carers may have expectations that children will be able to do certain things at certain stages, particularly as regards phonology – for example, that they will be able to pronounce certain consonant clusters by a certain age. But even allowing for individual variation, this is unlikely to figure largely in any child's awareness of language.

Children whose environment contains two languages are in a somewhat different position. They are much more likely to be aware of 'Language' itself, especially if they are acquiring two or more languages. This awareness can become manifest in three ways:

- at the level of different language systems

- at the level of different language status, and

- in different levels of language development.

Firstly, the two languages being acquired may be systematically different. One may rely heavily on word-order as a carrier of meaning: 'the dog bit the man' uses the same words as 'the man bit the dog', but the meanings are quite different, depending on which is the subject and which the object. The other might use a system of inflections on nouns and verbs to convey the meaning that one word in an utterance is the subject of a verb and another word the object. Children who encounter two languages that differ thus in their internal system are faced immediately with linguistic difference, and must solve the problem in order to 'crack the semantic code' (Kamiol, 1990:151).

Secondly, the potential bilingual will become aware of different users of language and will discover that languages do not all share the same status. Hamers and Blanc (1982) have argued that if children's language is systematically reinforced in the community by the presence of other speakers, by roadsigns, shop signs, literature and other media, they gain a significant wash-back effect which enhances their confidence, self-identity and, thus, acquisition. If, however, this feedback is absent and their language is marginalised, is not represented in the school system or other institutions, and is spoken only in low-status environments, this beneficial effect is lost. For children acquiring two languages, the question of the languages' differential status will be relevant. Language can be seen, by others and by the self, as a badge of personal and social identity, and as one of the fault lines in society, revealing where divisions and tensions lie.

The third measure of variation is the stage of language development. Clearly children acquiring two or more languages simultaneously, or even successively, are unlikely to have developed balanced competence in both by the age of entry into school. This means that they may enter school with relatively poor skills in both languages as compared to a monolingual norm or they may have good skills in only one of the languages. In either case, children may well become aware of the difference between themselves and others' language levels.

Expectations: Literacy, Oracy and Culture

Certain strong expectations about the world outside the home and crucially about school will already have been set by the age of 4 or 5. A critical one will be about literacy.

There is clearly great diversity of literacy practices in homes, ranging from those in which reading is very limited to those in which it seems almost to be a full-time occupation. Reading may be almost entirely instrumental. Adults may use it mainly for finding out about TV programmes or checking out the sports pages of newspapers. Others may find pleasure in extensive discursive reading, seeing it as a way their culture is transmitted and insisting that children become competent readers. There is a long continuum of reading practice between these extremes, relating to levels of adult literacy, levels of education, occupation and personal motivation and interest. But whatever the practice is in the home, it will inevitably affect the children brought up in it in two principal ways.

Firstly, the attitude towards literacy will vary. There are considerable contrasts among cultures in attitudes to reading and texts. Some cultures value reading mainly as access to religious and spiritual truths, and these truths may be expressed in a language remote from everyday discourse. This is the case for Muslims, whose home language could be one of many, but whose language of literacy may only be the Arabic of the Qur'an. This stands in stark contrast to an English monolingual child who is encouraged to see reading as fun and as a skill that has to be acquired.

Secondly, the practice and the mechanics of reading will vary. Adults from any culture may see reading as vital for their children even when they themselves are not fluent readers. They may have strong views about how children best acquire the reading skill. (See Gregory, 1997 for an examination of cultural attitudes to literacy.)

Thus when literacy is looked at from within a single culture, or across several, there is huge scope for differences in attitudes to, and competence in, reading and writing. It is inevitable that children coming to school for the first time will have absorbed or been explicitly instructed in a particular attitude or skill acquisition, or both.

We have taken literacy here as one example of the potential differences in expectations about schooling in a community. It would be equally possible to look at the different expectations about oracy. We have already suggested that parents have ideas about the stages of development in talk, about politeness expressed in vocabulary and terms of address; about turn-taking, silence, conversational partners, times for talking, and so on. As complex as the (only partial) picture is so far, it becomes far more so when we consider children who have been in school for two or three years. Older children may be experiencing the pull of the peer-group alongside the pull of the home, each demanding conformity but each with its own set of norms. All children are in this position. No child speaks or behaves in exactly the same way at home as they do at school. But where different languages and cultures are concerned and where members of the family are competent in different languages, children can be seen to be in a tense intermediate position, and may even find themselves acting as an intermediary between two cultures.

Diversity in Children Learning English as an Additional Language

Children coming to school for the first time who have been exposed to a language or languages other than English, can be characterised to some extent by combinations of the following:

- They may be perceived by others as representing a coherent group of children – eg 'from the Indian sub-continent'. Such loose labelling will certainly mask the real diversity of culture and language. Labels denoting ethnicity, language and religion can be confused. Within any one class, school or even ethnic group, a number of first languages may be represented, though certain languages may predominate.

- They may have had, and continue to have, differing levels of exposure to their additional language.

- As individuals they have differing levels of *uptake* from their additional language. We cannot assume that just because a language is available to a certain child it will be acquired at the same rate as by another child – any more than in the case of two monolinguals. Some bilingual children come to school with English indistinguishable from that of their monolingual peers whereas others have very little English. And even where the level of English is similar to that of a monolingual, we cannot assume that the child's culture-based expectations are the same as those of a monolingual.

- They will have different levels of competence in their home language. Indeed, the position in respect of the home language can vary as greatly as that for the additional language. What is key from the educational point of view is that the capacity of the home language is likely to go unmeasured. Sometimes this is because there is no-one who can give an informed assessment; sometimes it is because the school does not see the value of such assessment. There is strong evidence, however, that a high level of competence in the home language is a good predictor of subsequent educational success. Moreover, if one accepts Cummins' (1996) argument, competence in the home language will accelerate the child's conceptual development regardless of whether that is articulated through the language(s) of home or of school.

These are some of the important factors that will apply to any child learning EAL when they enter the English school system for the first time. Next, we look at the situational factors in the school that are relevant to children's acquisition of English.

The history of how the English system has reacted to the presence of large numbers of children learning EAL is documented in Townsend (1970) for early responses, and later, Reid (1988). The current position is that children are almost exclusively in the mainstream rather than withdrawn from classes for any purpose, on the grounds the National Curriculum is an access curriculum from which no-one can be excluded. The view is widely held that natural interaction between children is likely to promote the acquisition of English more than separation into purely language-based classes. Paradoxically, however, although the National Curriculum lays great stress on English, it puts little on language.

It is always dangerous to think of a curriculum without considering the people to whom it has to be mediated. A curriculum that is designed in terms of desirable outcomes – what pupils should be able to 'do' at the end – is particularly dangerous if one ignores where the pupils are starting from. So, while it may in itself be desirable that all pupils should, at the end of Key stage 1, for example, be 'introduced to the some of the features that distinguish standard English' (DfEE, 1995: 5), the means of arriving at that outcome may differ from one set of pupils to another. Specifically, those whose level of English differs significantly from that of their peers are likely to benefit from explicit attention to what they already know about and can do with language. Pupils who are learning a language and a curriculum together are less likely to succeed when the skills, knowledge and expectations about language they developed before they came to school are ignored. However new the curriculum may be to the child, the child is never a clean slate.

The diversity of language/s among EAL learners may or may not be shared by members of school staff or specialist support staff. Social background and language practice are also diverse. Some families, for example, encourage children to acquire at a community school a language which has a purely religious role (Qur'anic Arabic), perhaps alongside a standard form of a language of which they speak a vernacular form in the home. There is diversity in the levels and types of literacy in the home. Some parents are not literate in English and the role of supporting literacy in English may fall to siblings, who may themselves be at the intersection of two sets of practice – those that obtain in home-language literacy classes and those of the mainstream school (Gregory and Williams, 1998). So even before children enter the mainstream class, they have been exposed to a range of influences on their language and literacy development, of which the school may have little knowledge. Fundamentally, they will have become used to certain ways of expressing their meanings. This raises the critical question of context.

The Primary School as a Second Language Learning Context

How do schools measure up as places in which to learn that additional language? Do they provide a naturalistic or a tutored environment for second language acquisition? Is there an explicit language syllabus, purposely designed materials, regular set times for language learning, specific discrimination between skills, explicit instruction about the aims of the language-learning task? Or are EAL learners more or less immersed in the second language, offered little structured learning, and compelled to make use of every communicative trick at their disposal to 'hack into' the language somehow? Are the children expected to remember appropriate fragments, to analyse them in some way, to see what works and what doesn't, and ultimately to recombine the fragments in novel and effective utterances in the correct context?

There is unlikely to be a school where a 'pure' form of either of these learning modes operates. But we can learn a good deal from these extreme models when we look at the circumstances in which EAL learners in English schools are expected to acquire English.

One important element is how explicitly language is focused on and taught. Clearly, learners will benefit from almost any language instruction or explicit talk about language but the sharper the focus, the better. As in all teaching, the more accurately the work is directed at the learners, the more comprehensible it is likely to be (see Krashen, 1982 for the role of 'comprehensible input in' second language learning). The question is whether the kind of language-work such learners are given is best designed to facilitate their rapid acquisition of high levels of English.

We have already noted that the National Curriculum, although strong on English, says little about language. English is the only language that the school system has a responsibility for developing, and while the existence of accents is acknowledged (DfEE, 1995: 5), this is the only variation permitted from a unitary model of language. The difficulty with this is that if teachers are to think about language at all, there is no encouragement to do so except through the way in which English works as a language. Teachers are given no ways of seeing language except through the prism of English, and this can affect how they see children with a first language other than English.

A further factor is the relationship between the 'Englishes' of pupils and the variety that schools are charged with developing – standard English. Most children in schools will share a good number of the 'core' features of English, such as syntax and basic vocabulary. Every speaker of English, from wherever in the world, will put together sentences in the order subject-verb-object – there is no other possibility. This fundamental 'formula' is arguably the single most powerful bond holding together all existing varieties of English. And the vocabulary children use to refer to everyday objects, regularly seen television programmes and characters and so on, will probably be very similar among all English monolingual children, regardless of their social background.

I have just offered a very 'top-down' view of language, one that sees the essential regularities of the system rather than the idiosyncrasies of usage. It privileges those aspects of language that 'conform', rather than those that are culturally marked. So, whilst a linguist might make generalisations about varieties of English and point out their common patterns and constraints (eg in syntax), it is a different matter for a learner whose everyday experience is linguistic variety and to whom the common patterns are invisible precisely because they are embedded in everyday discourse. What is salient to a novice learner of a language is the differences in the way it is spoken – different accents and specific vocabulary which are heavily marked culturally and even locally.

So while some working-class English children (and parents) with strong local accents may recognise that 'school' English will deviate from their own, children learning English as an additional language have less robust models of English in the home, may be insecure in core aspects of syntax, formation of tenses, complex sentences, use of the verb to be, and so on and have an uncertain conception of what English is like. This applies not just in terms of a system whose mechanics need to be internalised for them to be able to produce rapid, error-free language but also to English as a set of cultural norms. It is the hidden meanings, the cultural pragmatics of the language that have to be acquired as well as its more open, 'inspectable' workings. NALDIC (1998:5) makes this clear in relation to literacy:

> Pupils learning EAL will not have the same range and experience of English language in context as native speakers. They will need to learn about the cultural references in texts to be able to understand the meaning. They will also require support in understanding:
>
> • inferential language and allusions embedded in texts
> • differential meanings of words in context
> • constructions used in particular genres
> • metaphorical use of language
> • culturally embedded language
> • use of dialect forms

The same can equally well be said about speech. Specific topics in the English curriculum fail to take this issue into account. At Key stage 1 (age 5-7), children are expected to be familiar with the conventions of 'discussion and conversation, eg taking turns in speaking' and teachers are urged to encourage children to 'listen with growing attention and concentration, to respond appropriately and effectively to what they have heard' (DfEE, 1995:4). Thus relatively new emphasis on the structure of language (NALDIC, 1998:10) is not itself unhelpful for language development but without a knowledge of where the children are starting from, they are largely empty categories. Crucially, they will not equip teachers with the knowledge to deliver good education. Based as they are on erroneous assumptions about a homogenous English language population, they are contrary to constructive approaches to learning English as a second language.

The school environment may be unhelpful to EAL learners' language development for another reason: the misplaced focus on difference – difference in stage of language development and difference in knowledge of the target code. This approach ignores all the language development that is going on in the children's first language – as do all the official documents.

It is important to be realistic. Children enter primary schools equipped with productive skills in their first language that may range from minimal ability to full competence. Teachers rarely know much about this because assessment of children in their first language is patchy and irregular. But first language development is significant for a number of reasons, even if children's productive skills are still poor.

For a start, the child's first language would be the primary means of socialisation, with all the implications this has for personal and social identity. It may be the majority language of discourse in the home or community, and the sole language of discourse for some people in the home, such as grandparents. It may be the language in which these hidden meanings are embedded; that is, the language in which jokes, stories, proverbs, allusions and metaphors are communicated – a topic to which I will return. We know that receptive capacity to language is well in advance of production for all children, so even when children cannot produce language fluently, they cannot be regarded as being cut off from this vital source of cultural meanings. Finally, the mother tongue may well be a badge of identity: children may regard themselves as a member of one particular language community.

To sum up the arguments: primary schools are not ideal language-learning environments for children learning English as an additional language because of the narrow focus on English and because a curriculum based on English for monolinguals cannot possibly be taught in a way that takes account of the linguistic and conceptual categories already laid down in children's first language.

An Introduction to the Study

Clearly, bilingual children in schools do not form a homogenous population. So we need to be sensitive and imaginative in determining what their language capacities are, rather than making assumptions based on inadequate assessments. The transcripts that follow show that:

- oral production from children (conversation, narrative) is an excellent means of assessing linguistic competence and that

- surface error, as it appears in speech, can be insignificant when compared to a holistic, 'larger picture' of a child's language ability.

Accordingly, support should be differentiated according to actual needs.

• Informants and Data

The data presented here consists of naturalistically collected material emerging from interviews at school with two children from the same language background. The first example is a pair of narratives on the same topic, the second a narrative deriving from a previously written text. In each case the data is presented first, followed by an analysis which aims to demonstrate the contrast between surface error and larger, more overarching language skills.

Figure 1 shows relevant facts about each informant and the language sample taken from each.

Figure 1: Informants, discourse types and topics

Informant	Age	Gender	L1	Years in UK	Type of discourse	Topic
1. (data set 1a and 1b)	10	male	Sylheti	10	narrative	Schools in Bangladesh
2. (data set 2)	10	female	Sylheti	10	narrative from written source	A magic journey under-ground

• Data Set 1 (a and b)

Data-set 1 (texts a and b) consists of two short narratives about school life in Bangladesh. The audience was an English researcher, familiar to the informant but not sharing his mother tongue.

text a

There was a school far .... from about one mile further than our house. In this school me and my bro.... brother used to read first. The teacher.. wasn't so ... kind and he al.... was sleepy always. He .. he was always telling us to read and he went to sleep. One day he went to sleep while we were playing games. We played games ... we made we p-playing with papers and throw at him. He was so angry that he woke up and chased us all. Then we all went home. The next day....the sir wasn't there again .... he was ....he w... he went to London and he didn't came back for about two three years.

text b

There was once a school, next to my uncle's house. Me and my brother used to read there. And one day a girl was reading next to my brother .... sitting next to my brother. Then the man ....the teacher said to him... her .....to read a poem, but she couldn't so the teacher tried to hit her .....[interruptions] The teacher tried to hit her with a ruler but she moved away and he fall on my brother's leg. My brother was crying. [interruptions] and he feel ....and he .....the teacher felt sorry for him and he went home. So the next day the girl brought his brother with her and his brother got some friends with him and they all .....make the teacher feel sorry.

Focus of Analysis for Data Set 1 (text a)
Table 1: errors in text a by type

	lexical	grammatical	word order	deictic
1	far			
2				further than our house
3			first	
4	wasn't so kind			
5			was sleepy always	
6		we playing with papers		
7		[we] throw at him		
8	the sir			
9	again			
10	two three years			

Table 2: organisation of text a by clause

Clause	Main verb	Co-ordinate or sub-ordinate verb	Clause function
1	there was		scene-setting
2	used to read		background action
3	wasn't so kind		character description
4	was always telling us to read	and he want to sleep	habitual/typical action
5	went to sleep	while we were playing	foreground action + background action
6	played games		foreground action
7	made		false start
8	playing with papers	and throw at him	continuous actions
9	was so angry	that he woke up and chased	main action + results
10	went home		foreground action
11	wasn't there		foreground action
12	was		false start
13	went to London	and didn't come back	foreground actions

This brief analysis focuses on the informant's awareness and exploitation of a narrative form in which to tell his story. Table 1 shows a classification of the perceived errors made by the speaker and Table 2 shows the way in which the text can be seen to be organised by clauses.

Discussion

Table 1 shows no particular pattern. The informant makes a small, if noticeable, number of errors of four types, none of which impedes comprehension. The lexical errors are minor – little more than questions of usage. The grammatical errors are inconsistent: 'we playing', where the auxiliary 'were' is omitted, can be countered by 'we were playing games', showing that the informant does have this form available. Both errors of word order concern adverbs, notorious as the most mobile element of the English sentence. The deictic error – the uncertainty about the usage of 'far' and 'further' – is not uncommon in monolinguals of this age.

Contrast these with the analysis in Table 2. Simply reading the whole of text 1 gives an impression of a well thought-out and well-organised narrative, and the impression is based on good evidence. The informant has a clear view of background and foreground actions, and consistently uses tense and aspect to articulate the relation between them: continuous forms for the former, simple past for the latter. This ability to organise levels of information is a major factor in the clarity of the story. There are occasional lapses of form ('throw at him' in clause 8, where the target is 'throwing [them] at him'), even though, as we noted in discussing Table 1, the continuous form is well established.

There is significant contrast between surface error and 'the big picture'. When we assess children who are learning a second language, we may be predisposed to notice error. It is important to look just as carefully at the higher levels of language – in this case, narration. In this example we see that the overall organisation of the text is matched almost perfectly by a linguistic system of tenses that vividly conveys meaning.

The same types of analysis work equally well in the case of the second text, given here to demonstrate the consistency of the informer's strategies and competence, but not analysed.

• *Data – set 2*

The context of the narrative collected from the second informant is rather different. It is an 'oralised' version of a story that she had previously produced as a piece of written text under the title 'A magic journey underground'. So whereas the first informant was producing his narrative without preparation and thinking on his feet, the second informant is re-working, again in real time, a text to which she has already given a good deal of thought.

There is not space here to produce the full text. In summary, the informant (writing in the first person) wakes up one fine morning and wants to go straight outside. Her mother forbids her, sending her off to tidy her room before she's allowed out. Alone and bored, she notices a crack in the wall and digs away at it, uncovering a secret passage, stairs, an underground room and finally a wonderful banquet. Having eaten her fill, she turns the journey into a dream, and wakes up.

If we relate this narrative to those of the previous informant, we find even greater clarity of narrative structure and effective allocation of verb-forms to actions and descriptions. Technically, there are very few problems, none worth discussing here. Instead, we will turn to another aspect of language which is arguably more demanding and receives less attention in schools than the usual run of grammatical technicalities.

Literal and Non-literal Language

Linguists make a distinction between literal and non-literal language, between language used for simply 'referring to' things and its more subtle uses. What does this mean for children learning EAL? Halliday's early work (eg Halliday, 1975) looks at language as a way of constructing meaning. He claims that the first thing children 'do' with language is to name things and people around them. Language is initially a means of labelling the world and thus rendering it knowable and manageable – a child's early vocabulary consists of words used with a literal meaning. A sock is a sock and nothing else.

But as the pragmatic ability of the child develops, in parallel with sophisticated linguistic systems such as syntax and phonology (Foster, 1990), words cease to be simple labels and gain social or inter-personal significance. Thus, to somebody who shares the meaning-world of the child, the word 'sock' may indicate not just a sock that is present in the space they share but may refer to a joint experience in which a sock figured – a joke about a sock, or a time when they couldn't find the sock. And this can be seen as the beginning of the development of the child's non-literal language skill – the ability to see words as not tied only to a particular context but as allusions to something else. It is the start of jokes, proverbs, idioms, similes and the whole range of metaphorical language. Inherent in it is the child's ability to accept that a word refers to more than one thing, and that a referent can be expressed by one or more different labels according to speaker, context and the communicative effect the speaker wants to have.

According to these variables, the same 'thing' might be referred to – sometimes even by the same speaker – as 'the corpse', 'the deceased', 'the late Ms Flint', 'Aunty' and 'the stiff in the parlour'. The language of a child without a capacity to use words this way would seem curiously flat and monotonous and there is an interesting connection with the language of autistic individuals, who do have difficulty with non-literal modes of speech (Jordan and Powell, 1995: 82-86).

Focus on the Analysis for Data-set 2

Returning to our informants, we must bear in mind that their early socialisation, crucially carried through language, is likely to have been rich in this use of language, but not necessarily in English. While the metaphorical use of language is universal, it is also deeply specific to individual cultures, each of which is a kind of prism through which its members see the world.

Similes are a good example. English natives characteristically associate certain qualities with certain animals – bravery with lions, stubbornness with donkeys, fatness with pigs (but thinness with rakes ...). Acquiring this repertoire of ready-made similes is part of growing up; it is pre-fabricated knowledge that we can bring into use at any time. If we are tired of it, we can refresh it by making changes but we do so against the background knowledge in the mind of our audience that we are making a conscious change. This kind of intimately transmitted knowledge includes a whole invisible range of cultural references, inferences and assumptions. The point is that it is extremely difficult to acquire from the outside, one reason being that it is difficult to 'see'. We don't know when we 'teach' it to children, or in what context. We simply do it, and they somehow know it.

Discussion

It is useful to extract from the informant's narrative a number of words and phrases and consider them in their immediate context. Most significant is the use of metaphorical language, indicated in Table 3 by the categories 'phrase' and 'lexis'. Another feature is indicated by the category 'tactic', which refers to what looks like an acquired discourse strategy that the informant is using to organise her text. Finally, we comment on 'position': the positioning of adverbs in their clause (a comparative link with a feature of the first informant's performance).

Without the full text of this story, it is difficult to give a flavour of the full range of ability evidenced by this EAL learner. It is all the more important to stress the degree to which she internalised the English linguistic system in order to have arrived at this level of performance.

Her use of non-literal language, instanced in the 'phrases' in Table 3, is impressive. Phrases like these do not necessarily indicate particular imaginative capacity. For the native English learner who has reached a certain competence, they probably represent 'islands of reliability' – more-or-less fixed units that can be brought into action

Table 3: Informant's language use in data-set 2 by category

		Category		
Example	**Phrase**	**Lexis**	**Position**	**Tactic**
the sun's rays burning on my window	X			
I quickly got up			X	
meekly		X		
with slime dripping in certain places	X			
chamber		X		
from place to place	X			
I suddenly grew tired			X	
a table groaning with the weight of food	X			
so I tucked myself in	X			
this is going to be a nice lunch		X		
sleepy, sleepy				X
suddenly I woke up				X

to render a text more 'interesting' in the eyes of a teacher. Intriguingly though, the EAL learner gets two or three of them slightly wrong. There is something not quite right about 'the sun's rays burning *on* my window'. Is the target 'burning *through* my window'? Then 'slime dripping in certain places' seems a bit weak, as though the narrator hadn't quite found the right term. And 'I *tucked myself* in' is a combination of two idioms, 'tucking into a meal ' and '[being] tucked up in bed'.

Related to this use of language are the terms identified in Table 3 under 'lexis'. These are signs that the language-user is consistently trying – not always successfully – to go beyond simply 'denoting' certain everyday objects, events or feelings, towards a more expanded linguistic repertoire. There is evidence of potential as well as of performance.

The second, lesser, point is her ability to manipulate a discourse routine. The topic demands a narrative with several episodes and an element of surprise. The informant's response is a clear three-part structure with a beginning set in everyday reality, a fantastic and imaginative centre, and a return to the everyday at the end. Within this structure, she uses two narrative 'tactics' to carry her through the transition from one episode to another – the falling asleep and sudden awakening at the end. Thus 'sleepy....... ' (repeated several times in a dying tone on the tape), and the phrase 'suddenly I woke up', while not imaginative, indicate that she can control acquired discourse devices in order to organise her text.

Implications for Support

Children like those discussed here will gain from strong linguistic support. The first prerequisite of support is for teachers to know the children's language and cultural background. Without knowledge of the world in which the learners have their roots, and especially of the 'prism' through which the world of the school is viewed, we do not know what we are supporting. For the National Curriculum to be truly an access curriculum, it must provide a level playing field for all. Equal opportunities means not that all children are equally well endowed, whether with intelligence or material wealth, but that each individual has comparable opportunities to take advantage of what the system can provide.

Secondly, we have to examine the language of bilingual children at a number of levels. There is considerable diversity across local education authorities in the UK and government-funded support projects in assessing language (Rea-Dickinson and Gardner 1998). Over time these have moved, in line with developments in language assessment elsewhere, from structural concerns to more pragmatic/ functional ones – towards seeing what the child can do with language. In fact both levels are significant, and they interact with each other.

When we look at a text-type such as a narrative, we need to see how each child is coping with both the macro task of narrating a story and the micro level of accuracy in tenses and so on. Both the EAL learners discussed here had high-level skills of narration, that is, control over structure and episode, plus the ability to express individual actions or descriptions within each episode by accurately using tense and aspect. It is important to look at what each learner can do before searching out lapses or gaps in competence.

Thirdly, oracy is important. With the recent stress on developing literacy, it can be forgotten that speech underlies the development of reading and writing skills. Children learning English as an additional language may only be able to articulate certain aspects of language in speech. Thus, for example, the demands of writing either of the two short narratives given here (data-set 1) would have been far beyond what was required to produce them orally. But without the opportunity to produce them orally, we would not have discovered the first child's capacity to construct narratives and his ability to use tense and aspect to good effect. While this is true for all children, it is particularly true for the children about whom I am writing, for whom the gap between speech and writing may be wider than for their peers.

Finally, a broad and rich language curriculum for learners of additional languages, one that includes attention to non-literal language, is essential. We have seen how one EAL learner manages to absorb, recall and utilise aspects of English metaphor and use them accurately, if slightly oddly. She has been able to penetrate the code of English at a metaphorical level and make sense of it; to retain the forms and meanings and re-use them appropriately. We need to be sure that children have access to the full range of the language's potential. Access should mean more than access to a common core of syntax and vocabulary. Children need to become aware of the hidden meanings of the language, the inferences and allusions that remain embedded in culturally loaded text. Without an understanding of these, no speaker can be a fully competent user of a language.

This is not to argue that children learning EAL must become just like native speakers. Lengthy debate in the field of English language teaching over the status of the native speaker (Rampton, 1990; Davies, 1991; Widdowson, 1993) has concluded that native speakers are not best at everything in their mother tongue. They do better on tests of grammatical accuracy but no better than non-native speakers on tests of comprehension. Moreover, non-native speakers are more flexible in their interpretation of English, allowing a greater range of possible meanings to arise from a given utterance.

Ultimately, while we would want all children to have comparable levels of comprehension and production of language, the differences between them should ideally relate rather to individual characteristics than to differences of mother tongue. We would not want children to be without the special perspective on the world afforded them by their membership of other speech communities. Chinua Achebe rejected the notion that writing in English would prevent him from expressing the reality of Africa. But he rejected equally the notion that it would be anybody's English but his own:

> I feel that the English language will be able to carry the weight of my African experience. But it will have to be a new English, still in communion with its ancestral home but altered to suit its new African surroundings. (Achebe, 1965:222)

This seems a good goal for the language education of children learning EAL too.

Bilingual Teaching in a Russian-Finnish Class

Anna Hirvonen

Myllypuro Comprehensive School, Helsinki, Finland

The Project

A bilingual Russian-Finnish first class has been established at Myllypuro Lower Stage Comprehensive School as part of an EU project to be implemented in the cities of Helsinki, Espoo and Vantaa. The objective is to develop the teaching and evaluation of immigrant schoolchildren. The project began in the school when a model of bilingual teaching was developed in co-operation with the teachers of the Leipuri daycare centre, a bilingual pre-school group, and various other parties. As part of the project, the daycare centre was developing a bilingual pre-school teaching model of its own at the time.

Linguistic objectives and objectives related to the self-confidence and identity of the pupils were formulated for class activities. The aim of the teaching was to maintain and develop the pupils' first language skills, since children's native language must be developed as the vehicle for learning and abstract thinking. If Finnish is the only teaching language, the pupils' skills in both their own language and their second language could remain superficial, and this would impede their learning. Learning their own language would support Russian-speaking children in learning Finnish, and deficient language skills and underachieving could be avoided. In this way stress that interferes with learning and aggravated by not knowing the language of instruction sufficiently well is reduced, and the children's self-confidence and identity strengthened.

The main emphasis is placed on linguistic objectives. Intensive teaching is given in both the pupils' first language and Finnish for at least the first two years of school, and monitoring is carried out to see how intensive mother tongue teaching and support by an adult with the same native language helps the children's school work, their learning of Finnish and learning in general. At the same time the pupils' bilingual identity is reinforced, and they are encouraged to use their first language in a variety of situations.

The daycare centre began supporting Russian-speaking children in their first language and providing intensive teaching in the Finnish language. The Leipuri daycare centre has a bilingual pre-school group with a pre-school teacher and assistant, both of whom are bilingual in Finnish and Russian. The aim was to place the entire pre-school group in the bilingual class of the Myllypuro Lower-Stage School, which, with the exception of a few pupils, was done. A few new pupils from other pre-school groups joined the group. There were eleven Russian-speaking and thirteen Finnish-speaking pupils in the class. One of the Finnish-speaking pupils had a hearing impairment and one Russian-speaking pupil came from a group of dysphasic children.

There are two teachers, one Finnish-speaking and one Russian-speaking. The Russian-speaking children receive six hours a week of instruction in the Russian language in their own group, covering their native language, mathematics and science. The two teachers give an additional ten hours of instruction a week together. The subject material discussed in the native-language classes is repeated during the joint lessons. This guarantees that the Russian-speaking pupils learn the concepts discussed in Finnish, too. The Finnish-speaking class teacher handles arts, crafts and music classes alone. The Russian-speaking pupils have one hour a week of instruction in Finnish as a second language.

The importance of the mother tongue teacher is not restricted to pupil contact. It is also important for the teacher to be able to communicate with the parents, which requires more than language skills.

The teacher has to be able to act as an interpreter between cultures, to explain to the immigrant parents what the practices and objectives of Finnish schools are when these differ from those in their country of origin, and to interpret to the Finnish teachers what the parents expect from the school.

The bilingual class in school is thus an integrated group with as many Finnish-speaking as Russian-speaking pupils. We consider it vital for the children to be able to establish contact in natural circumstances and to form friendships across languages; the Russian children must be provided with naturally occurring free-form situations for learning Finnish. Since the Russian children are likely to move over to purely Finnish-language teaching from the third year, they must become accustomed to instruction given in Finnish during the first two years of school to prepare them. It is also important that all children feel they belong together and are not separated and treated as different groups that cannot work together.

Although the Russian-Finnish class is called bilingual, this is not quite so; there is no objective that Finnish-speaking children should learn Russian. But a Russian club has been organised for Finnish children who are interested in becoming acquainted with the Russian language.

The language skills, learning and social development of the pupils was evaluated in pre-school with material developed by the Portti working group. As well as evaluation taking place within the curriculum, a researcher is to be hired for the job to evaluate the learning of the Russian-speaking pupils and document the benefits gained through intensified instruction in mother tongue.

The project's bilingual experiment has been going on for six months now. It is a short time, and the work we do is constantly modified by the experiences gained in the process. So far the experience has certainly been extremely positive.

The Russian children like to attend the classes in their own language group, since they experience success there and can talk about their own affairs and express themselves without difficulty. They benefit greatly from the presence in school of an adult who speaks their own language. When the children can turn to an adult who shares their language, adaptation becomes less problematic and the stress of starting school is noticeably reduced. There are many immigrant children in our schools so there are always plenty of children who speak the same language and a reference group with the same first language can always be found. However, more is needed: for small children this arrangement does not make up for an adult who can fully understand them. The Russian pupils in the bilingual class use their language boldly, knowing there will be no rejection of their own background or language – not the case for many Russian school children in Finland. Parents, too, have understood the importance of developing the children's mother tongue.

The pupils are learning their own language effectively, when compared with experiences from earlier school years. By the end of the first three months we had already reached the level previously reached by Russian pupils after the whole school year.

The differences between Russian and Finnish have not significantly affected the children's progress. A distinct difference between the two languages is the alphabet: Russian uses the Cyrillic alphabet, Finnish the Latin. A different letter may be used for one and the same sound in the two languages, or the same letter may stand for two different sounds (eg. the Cyrillic 'b' in Russian stands for the Latin 'v' in Finnish, and the Cyrillic 'p' stands for the Latin 'r'). In spite of this, the pupils do not make many mistakes; they can associate the right alphabet with the right language.

Learning to read and write has proceeded at the same rate in both languages, although it is more difficult to write Russian than Finnish. Russian words are longer and word stress is reflected in the orthography. Russian also has sounds that Finnish does not (for instance seven different 's' sounds), and distinguishing between them is difficult for Russian children living in a Finnish language environment. One special feature of their lessons in Russian is learning to use handwriting straight away, whereas Finnish children learn to write in small block letters. Handwriting is a more difficult motor process but any difference evens out as soon as Finnish-language handwriting begins. Then the Russian children actually have the advantage.

The number of hours taught in Russian in the bilingual class is triple that of the ordinary first language teaching offered by the National Board of Education and, significantly, the Russian-speaking teacher is present and co-teaches during the classes held for the whole group.

Perhaps the greatest benefit to the Russian children is the opportunity they have to go through a variety of subjects in their first language classes without having to concentrate only on reading and writing. When the class discussed the human being, for instance, the Russian-language class went through the names of the parts of the human body that they did not know in Russian.

If no such input is made, full understanding and command of one's first language is impossible. Learning their mother tongue may also be held back by learning a second language without fluency in the first on which to build. Learning specific vocabularies for various topics and subjects, and having sufficient practice in expressing one's thoughts in one's own tongue are vital if a child's language is to develop into a language for thinking and to reach the level of abstract thinking.

Conclusion

A functioning bilingual capacity is the objective. We aim to enable all pupils to study Finnish as a school subject and understand curriculum instructions in Finnish whilst being fluent in Russian. Our aim is for the Russian pupils to read and write Finnish, to help them recognise Finnish structures, to expand their Finnish-language vocabulary, to teach them to understand the meanings of Finnish-language words, to help them express themselves through facial expressions and gestures, to practice various forms of theatrical expression in the Finnish language, and to help them use Finnish in their everyday lives through the development of their first language and planned second language teaching. Our small project has shown that if good language skills are acquired in Russian and Finnish during the early years of education, progress to higher order language skills in Finnish as a second language will be more secure and rapid than if taught without the support of their mother tongue. As a result of the project, this has become a central goal for teaching Finnish as a second language at lower comprehensive level .

Adaptation to Classroom Language

Maria Pinzani Tanini

Centro d'Iniziativa Democratica degli Insegnanti, Rome, Italy

In the complex spectrum of issues arising in Italy from the current migratory flow of non-European Union citizens, our national association of teachers, the Centro d'Iniziativa Democratica degli Insegnanti (CIDI), has been committed for several years to pursuing a goal which is crucial for the integration of immigrant children in our schools. I'm talking about language, in our case, the Italian language.

Over the past five years a range of different approaches and agendas has made it clear that, whatever a child's linguistic level or socialisation into Italian life, one of the principal issues for immigrant children's effective learning in school is the specific language of each curriculum subject.

The 700-word or so basic vocabulary required by children for their initial interaction and enabling them to communicate may be precisely the vocabulary that inhibits a high level of academic performance. This is because familiarity with this basic lexicon creates the illusion, even among teachers, that there is no language problem and they dismiss the very notion.

This applies right from the first years of primary school. Our work of research and ensuing action has focused on the textbook language of mathematics and geography designed for Primary Three, which in Italy concerns children age 7-8.

In the course of our work, expert teachers have conducted research in collaboration with the Department of Experimental Pedagogy of the Rome University 3. They soon realised that their research would also prove useful for Italian pupils having difficulty. As in the case of immigrant children, the poverty of their basic language – the language they have developed and use at home – is so far removed from the language of the school that they feel almost totally alienated by certain unfamiliar words. When we talk about poverty of language we do not just mean the vocabulary children use, the quantity or the quality of words. We mean the use of language itself – what am I communicating and why? We mean a lack of possibility or motivation to express thoughts or states of mind.

Where the language used in the family is sophisticated and extensive, children will learn more rapidly and become more familiar with the language of the school. The problem, then, is not so much 'being a foreigner' as living in conditions marginalisation and sociocultural poverty which, though often the conditions experienced by immigrant children, are not theirs alone. This is something which they and the fringe sectors of the autochthonous population have in common. Consequently the sphere of our research widened in response to the spectrum of potential users.

One of the greatest difficulties has been and remains the task of keeping teachers trained to meet the new demands. In Italy this is increasingly taking the form of 'assisted didactics'. The aim is to empower teachers to devise and utilise tests to ascertain linguistic nodes blocking a child's progress at school. However, diagnostic and recuperation activities are an integral part of the whole realm of individual attention for children and their overall living conditions (emotional, relational, cognitive) and for their overall learning environment.

The working hypothesis for the project is to foster a degree of integration that does not stop at merely tolerating the presence of foreign guests. In short, the aim is to welcome these children among us and to work first for their proper education and then for their cultural inclusion. The first priority is becoming increasingly clear. It is action to enable children to acquire a language base that is essential for their full participation in the didactic activities of the classroom.

We all know that to carry out any activity, knowledge of the language of work is vital. This is particularly true as regards learning and the school environment. We are still at the first stages in our efforts to devise adequate strategies to address this problem, which is largely new to us.

Who would be the most suitable candidates for building and verifying the necessary linguistic bases? It seems obvious to look to teachers of the mother tongue (at least in our Italian case). But the task is not about the routine teaching of Italian, dealing with the linguistic problems of autochthonous children. Instead, special didactic strategies must be elaborated to intervene adequately and develop children's linguistic skill in a language not their own. To a degree, teachers of Italian language will have to learn to work in the same way as foreign language teachers. It might seem strange but this approach appears highly useful in the case of autochthonous children who are in difficulty because dialect is spoken at home and in their general environment, and this inhibits their command of complex language structures.

In the course of our work, we have been able to pinpoint in the daily language of the school the degree to which linguistic scenarios may vary according to family environment, television or any other external stimulus. Each curriculum subject, oral test, lesson, group discussion or textbook constitutes a linguistic world of its own.

In short, complex problems of glotto-didactics arise. How are the various types of linguistic skills defined and how are they verified? How different is the oral code from the written? How does the new language interfere with the mother tongue? What are the differences between an active and passive vocabulary?

These questions are compounded by problems relating to the dimension of the curriculum subject concerned: common expressions, for example, may assume a totally different meaning when applied to arithmetic. The word 'problem' itself is commonly used for difficult situations, for complexities which, by definition, are either lacking in information for their solution or too packed with it for it to be solved every time. Then there is the mathematical 'problem' which, by definition, furnishes all the information we need to resolve it. Another loaded word is 'operation' (complicated operation, surgical operation, and so on) whereas an 'operation' in arithmetic is a procedure whereby two given numbers may have an univocal association. What didactic tools should be used to address this type of problem? How can we pinpoint objective information on the language of the school curriculum, especially for different groups of children?

These questions formed the basis of our research and action through the years; initially, our study was of a lexical-statistical and didactic-appraisal nature. Specifically, we analysed active and passive lexical abilities in the spheres of certain curriculum subjects, such as Maths and Geography, for 7-8 year olds. We studied textbooks and approaches to oral lessons (by recording a large number of lessons for children from various sociocultural and geographical environments).

The result was a corpus of about 200,000 word frequencies, which we analysed and entered into a computer program. This produced a series of word frequency dictionaries relative to the curriculum subjects under examination and the classes of reference. The dictionaries were categorised morphologically, by nouns, adjectives, verbs and so on. By a system of indexing, several word frequency packages were formulated as questionnaires/charts to verify linguistic understanding and language use. We then carried out experiments in classes with immigrant pupils and distributed the questionnaires/charts to all the pupils. The answers were tabulated and summarised for interpretation.

At this stage it seemed appropriate to start comparing the methodologies deployed by colleagues from other countries. The project envisages establishing groups of teachers or experts in linguistics and statistics to elaborate procedures for their application to European schools with different pedagogical and professional traditions.

We are currently observing the extensive use being made of our databases in identifying linguistic difficulties and especially the difficulties of autochthonous children, with the language of the school. We aim to offer the teachers who have voluntarily contributed to the research and action groups a series of new working methods by which to assess and gauge linguistic familiarity.

From this new perspective, and with newly developed skill in analysing textbooks and lexical repertoires, teachers will be able to appraise textbooks and other learning materials. They will be more attentive to their own use of language in their work and will be in a position to make continuous, not occasional, assessments of the full linguistic skills of their pupils which may not be apparent in the school environment.

There must be a constant focus on in-depth analysis and remediation, in terms of activities that will converge with the routine school curriculum. Teachers must make on-going assessments and set targets throughout the year and not rely on the summative assessments at the end of the school year. Teaching and assessment of language must be the responsibility of all teachers from all disciplines, regardless of their curriculum specialism. In other words a science teacher must teach not only science and the language of science, but must use science as a medium for teaching language.

An evident result is that not only individual teachers but also authors, publishers and school administrations will have improved means of assessment at their disposal. The challenge of the project is more than just ensuring that teachers and experts from different cultural and organisational contexts will join in a process of research. It also lies in identifying new prospects of reciprocal enrichment at European level and in generating cultural interaction between some still very diverse worlds.

We are often reminded that the similarities in and differences between peoples and cultures must be conceived as a whole and that their interaction produces a synthesis of positive change. The numerous attempts under way in Europe to develop intercultural projects are the best way of consolidating a culture of peace and of helping new generations to co-exist in constant and conscious interaction.

Teaching English as an Additional Language:
time for a productive synthesis

Susan Jaine

Freelance Education Consultant, London, UK

Between 1960 and 1985 we had a system – 'early Section 11'* – that worked well for some children starting to learn English as an additional language (EAL) but not for all pupils with EAL. So in 1985 we dismantled the system and replaced it with one based on a well-meaning but simplistic understanding of what pupils from ethnic minority groups needed. This new system works fairly well for the pupils who might properly be described as bilingual.

The present system, however, doesn't serve EAL beginners well. Moreover, it fails to differentiate between second-stage learners of EAL, low-key bilingual pupils (those whose ethnic heritage includes a language other than English but whose main language is English, and who sometimes find it difficult to achieve their full potential because they cannot use standard English competently for academic purposes), and pupils who are fluent bilinguals.

Spurred on by political pressure, schools in England are striving for all pupils to make demonstrable progress. A system which fails to meet the needs of all EAL learners inevitably makes such pupils less attractive to schools who are required to demonstrate through standardised tests that their pupils are learning. We should therefore strive for a synthesis of effective methods for meeting the needs of EAL beginners, improvers, low-key bilingual pupils and fully fluent bilinguals. We need to be clear about the position of each pupil on the continuum, and provide appropriately for the needs of each of these groups of bilingual learners.

Coherent provision would include specialist part-time EAL teaching for beginners, training for specialist EAL teachers, training on issues of language and learning for all teachers, continuing work on curriculum strategies which promote the language development and learning of all pupils and the development of pupils' first languages.

1960s-1985: 'Early Section 11'

Before 1965, there were high levels of migration into the UK from countries both inside and outside the Commonwealth. Ethnic minority communities experienced considerable discrimination and prejudice, and it was felt that cultural and linguistic differences were creating barriers to the integration of migrants into what was seen as a homogeneous, monolingual and monocultural society. Section 11 of the 1966 Local Government Act empowered the Home Secretary to pay grant to Local Authorities and other institutions to pay for extra staff '... in consequence of the presence within their areas of substantial numbers of immigrants from *the Commonwealth* whose language or customs differ from those of the community' (my italics).

At this time, schools were admitting numbers of 'ESL (English as a Second Language) pupils' – pupils from the Commonwealth and elsewhere – who spoke little or no English. Some were the children of people coming to the UK for short stays, for study or business; some the children of refugees and some were the children of economic migrants. In many schools and education authorities, so-called Section 11 teachers were employed in an attempt to meet the needs of these pupils. In the main, Section 11 teachers were required to work with all ESL pupils, not solely with those of proven Commonwealth birth or heritage.

Because the mainstream curriculum was delivered exclusively in English, it was thought that pupils without fluent command of English needed to learn it before they could tackle the mainstream curriculum. It was generally agreed that they needed special places where they could be taught English as a second language. Accordingly, these pupils were given full-time or part-time withdrawal ESL tuition, either in their schools or in specialist centres. In London, on-site provision was normally made for primary pupils, while secondary age pupils attended off-site specialist centres. Pupils were not in mainstream classrooms on a full-time basis until they had mastered 'the fundamentals' of English.

Because specialist teaching was offered, specialist ESL teachers were needed and this required specialist training. The RSA Diploma in the Teaching of English as a Second Language was established as the main professional specialist qualification. Consequently, the general view in schools was that mainstream teachers needed to know little, if anything, about ESL or about the target pupils – the job of teaching them was done mainly or entirely by specialists.

Costs and Benefits

It was clear almost from the start that there were problems with this system. Some pupils were inappropriately selected to receive ESL teaching: for example, they might be identified as 'needing help' because of their name or ethnicity alone. Equally, teachers might be selected to become ESL specialists for the wrong reasons – they couldn't cope with the demands of class teaching or because they were themselves members of an ethnic minority group.

The standards of ESL teaching varied: in the best cases it was efficient and clearly related to helping pupils to operate within the mainstream curriculum, but in the worst cases it offered little more than basic tuition in 'remedial reading'. Mainstream teachers in many schools knew very little about their ESL pupils, and there was seldom any attempt to make the mainstream curriculum responsive to the needs of non-native speakers of English. If pupils were taught in a full-time withdrawal situation it could be difficult to integrate them into the mainstream.

On the other hand, the benefits of the system are often overlooked from today's perspective. Specialist bases, whether on- or off-site, could provide a safe haven where ESL learners could meet and support each other. This was particularly important in secondary schools where there might be only a few new arrivals, who would have been isolated from others in a similar situation just when peer support would be crucial in helping them to settle in a new environment. The existence of specialist centres also provided a strong educational argument against 'ghetto-ising' or directing pupils to a particular school because '... there are lots of similar pupils in that school, so he/she can get help'. Specialist bases were efficient: they could offer coherent, focused ESL teaching programmes, so that pupils made rapid progress, and specialist teachers got to know their pupils well. In optimal situations, this in-depth knowledge was effectively disseminated to mainstream colleagues.

Post-1985: 'Romantic Bilingualism'

Following the publication of the Swann Report (DES, 1985) and the Calderdale Report (CRE, 1986), the way educationalists viewed and sought to meet the needs of pupils who did not speak English as their first language changed dramatically. In 1990 the Home Office undertook a review of Section 11 posts. Existing posts were cancelled from the end of March 1992, and from April 1992 the Home Office instead approved and funded applications for some 450 projects that aimed to provide equality of access to the mainstream Nation Curriculum for ethnic minority pupils. Most education projects concerned the needs of bilingual pupils, with particular emphasis on in-class support.

In September 1993 Parliament amended Section 11 of the Local Government Act 1966. The words 'substantial numbers of immigrants from the Commonwealth' were replaced by the words 'persons belonging to ethnic minorities'. From 1995 government funding was provided (GEST 16 – then GEST 11 and 7 in 1996/97 respectively) specifically to train mainstream teachers to help them identify and meet the needs of bilingual pupils.

While these changes to the system were taking place, and in large part because of them, the 'ESL pupils' in our schools became 'bilingual pupils'. Much ink was spilt on explaining that 'bilingual' in an educational context did not mean what it meant in everyday parlance but, instead: 'at present using a language other than English, but potentially able to speak, read and write English'. It was stressed that all pupils had an entitlement to the mainstream curriculum, therefore all pupils had to be provided for 'in the mainstream'. Teachers were strongly cautioned against withdrawing any pupil from any lesson for any reason. Some exceptions were allowed, for instance very brief induction courses for newly-arrived pupils who spoke little or no English. The specialist centres were no longer needed. Specialist teachers were not needed either. Specialist training was ended, and existing specialists were grouped in project teams and devolved to support bilingual pupils in mainstream classes.

Costs and Benefits

The new system has brought with it some clear benefits for target pupils. For a start, mainstream teachers are generally better informed about pupils who speak, or need to learn, English as an additional language. In the most responsive schools, at least some areas of the mainstream curriculum have been developed and differentiated in a genuine attempt to meet the learning needs of a wide spectrum of pupils. The introduction of a National Curriculum has been beneficial in leading mainstream teachers to rethink both content and teaching methods, and this rethinking has given an opportunity for teachers of EAL to raise issues related to the language and learning needs of pupils with poor command of English. Initiatives such as collaborative learning, partnership teaching and the use of key visuals have been developed and many of these have benefited monolingual pupils as well as additional language learners.

However, there are still problems. The need to learn English for pupils who do not yet speak it is masked by terminology: they may be potentially bilingual, but they do not yet have the competence to function in an English-speaking classroom environment. Attempts to teach English as an additional language solely through in-class support are inevitably inefficient – EAL specialists work with one or two pupils at a time, and no coherent input can be provided on how the English language works. Beginners are taking longer to reach 'take-off point'. This leads to frustration for them, for their families and for their mainstream teachers. Also, it can lead to invidious situations in which schools make a strong commitment to dialogue with parents and community groups, but when the latter plead for specialist teaching for beginners of EAL they are told that the professionals know best, and that what they are asking for is not right for their children.

Total dependence on in-class support creates other problems. Where this support is provided, it is generally targeted at absolute or near-beginners, so the needs of second-stage EAL learners and low-key bilinguals are unlikely to be met. In any case, support cannot realistically be provided in every lesson, so that – more often than not – first-stage learners of EAL are only given additional support in a few curriculum areas where the linguistic demands of the subject are thought to be particularly high. Mainstream teachers in areas other than these are effectively excluded from the benefits of collaborative work and dialogue with EAL specialists.

Specialist EAL teachers, in turn, have been de-skilled, devalued and discouraged. There is now no recognised postgraduate qualification in EAL and no education degree (BEd) or post-graduate teacher training programme with EAL as a main subject. Many initial teacher-training programmes barely touch on ways of meeting the needs of EAL learners, whatever their level of English. Nor is there a career structure for teachers who might wish to work in this field – indeed, there is little job security.

Finally, pupils who are identifiable members of an ethnic minority are assumed to have a first language other than English, and it is further assumed that they are all competent and committed users of this language. This attitude has been defined as 'romantic bilingualism' in an important article by Roxy Harris (1997):

> The term 'Romantic Bilingualism' will be taken to refer to the widespread practice, in British schools and other educational contexts, of attributing to pupils drawn from visible ethnic minorities an expertise in and allegiance to any community languages with which they have some acquaintance.

We do not at present distinguish between those ethnic minority pupils who are competent, committed users of a home language (or languages) and those who may have some acquaintance with another language but whose 'main language' is English, albeit not the English needed for success in school. Interestingly, these low-key bilinguals have much in common with monolingual English pupils.

Time for a Productive Synthesis

It is high time for us to re-examine what we are doing for and to ethnic minority pupils to devise a framework that works for all of them. Our schools contain four distinct groups of linguistic minority pupils. First, there are beginner learners of English as an additional language: pupils who speak a language or languages other than English but little or no English. Second, there are second-stage EAL learners. Third, there are low-key bilingual pupils whose ethnic heritage includes a language other than English, but for whom English is the main language. Finally, there are genuinely bilingual pupils who are competent users of English and another language or languages. We must be clear about the situation of each individual pupil and we must provide for the needs of each.

For genuinely bilingual pupils who are competent users of English and another language, we must look seriously at provision for the maintenance and development of their skills in that language, whatever it may be. This will be a sizeable task, given the number of languages – over 200 first languages are spoken in London alone – and the geographical distribution of the pupils concerned. However, developments in technology that facilitate distance learning should make provision feasible. Much work has been done in this area, notably in mainland Europe and in North America, from which we could learn.

For pupils who speak a language or languages other than English but little or no English, we must as a matter of urgency and fairness provide specialist part-time EAL teaching. Such part-time foundation teaching has been proven to give learners the rapid, focused start they need in order to become competent users of a new language, without isolating them from their peers. Part-time inclusion in the mainstream helps these pupils to see clearly what they need to learn and why. The provision of EAL foundation courses would entail the reintroduction of training leading to a recognised professional qualification for specialist EAL teachers. It would be important for foundation courses taught by specialists to be professionally evaluated, in order to ensure the maintenance of *high* teaching standards.

If beginner learners of EAL are to make satisfactory progress within the mainstream, there must also be training on issues of language and learning for all teachers, in terms of what is offered on both initial teacher training courses and in-service training. There must, moreover, be continuing research into and work on curriculum strategies that promote the language development of all pupils. Research currently in hand on how learning in general takes place could inform work in this area.

All these strategies will obviously benefit second-stage learners of EAL and also low-key bilinguals: pupils who have some acquaintance with a language other than English and are competent users of English for basic interpersonal communication (BICS), but who fall short of full cognitive academic language proficiency (CALP).

Specialist EAL teachers should have a leading role in identifying the specific needs of each of these learners, and in working with them within and (where appropriate) outside of the classroom to develop their competence in English. Tuition should focus on 'written subject-specific standard English for academic purposes' (Harris, 1997). Specialist teachers must also work very closely with mainstream colleagues, in order to ensure that issues related to language and learning are at the forefront of the agenda in all our classrooms.

*   **Note:** Section 11 – In the UK there was special government funding to meet the needs of 'immigrant' people from the Commonwealth, later referred to as the New Commonwealth and Pakistan. This was administered by the Home Office under Section 11 of the 1996 Local Government Act. It initially funded any activity which required additional provision to be made over and above that normally provided by Local Government and some voluntary organisations. It later became mainly focused on education and gradually the 'New Commonwealth' dimension was removed so that grant could be used for initiatives for all ethnic minorities. In 1998 the funding arrangements changed and are now administered by the Department for Education and Employment under the title of Ethnic Minority Achievement Grant and from 2000, the grant includes the currently separate funding for Travellers and is called the Ethnic Minority and Traveller Achievement Grant. – Ed.

Bibliography

Achebe, C. (1965) 'English and the African Writer', *Transition* 4 (18): 27–30

Argyraki, F. *et al* (1994) 'Education and Dispersion', *Educational Community* issue 28, Athens

August, D. and Hakuta, K. (eds) (1997) *Improving schooling for language-minority children: A research agenda.* Washington, DC: National Academy Press.

Baker, C. and Jones, S.P. (1998) *Encyclopedia of bilingualism and bilingual education.* Clevedon, UK: Multilingual Matters

Bartolomy, L. (1994) Beyond the methods fetish: Toward a humanizing pedagogy. *Harvard Education Review,* 64, 173-194

Bates, I. (1995) The competence movement: conceptualising recent research. *Studies in Science Education,* 25 (1995), pp.39-68

Bernstein, B. (1996) *Pedagogy, symbolic control and identity.* London, Taylor and Francis

Board of Studies, Victoria (1996) *ESL companion to the English CSF.* Victoria, Board of Studies

Bourdieu, P. (1991) *Language and symbolic power.* London, Polity Press

Bourne, J. (1989) *Moving into the mainstream: LEA provision for bilingual pupils.* Windsor, NFER-Nelson

California State Department of Education. (1985) *Case studies in bilingual education: First Year Report.* Federal Grant #G008303723

California Department of Education. (1996) *Teaching reading: A balanced, comprehensive approach to teaching reading in prekindergarten through grade three.* Sacramento: California Department of Education

Campbell, W.J. and McMeniman, M.M. (1985) *Bridging the language gap: ideals and realities to learning English as a second language* (ESL). Canberra, Commonwealth Schools Commission

Cashion, M. and Eagan, R. (1990) Spontaneous reading and writing in English by students in total French immersion: Summary of final report. *English Quarterly,* 22(1), 30-44

Chamot, A. U. and O'Malley, M. (1994) *The CALLA Handbook: Implementing the Cognitive Academic Language Learning Approach.* Reading, MA: Addison-Wesley

Chana, U., Edwards, V. and Walker, S. (1997) Calligrapher or keyboard operator? Multilingual wordprocessing in the primary school. *Multicultural Teaching* 16 (1): 39-42.

Chana, U., Edwards, V. and Walker, S. (1998) Hidden resources: multilingual word-processing in the primary school. *Race, Ethnicity and Education* 1(1): 49-61.

Christian, D. (1994) *Two-way bilingual education: Students learning through two languages* (Educational Practice Report No. 12). Washington, DC: Center for Applied Linguistics and National Center for Cultural Diversity and Second Language Learning

Christian, D., Montone, C.L., Lindholm, K.J., and Carranza, I. (1997) *Profiles in two-way immersion education.* Washington, DC: Center for Applied Linguistics and Delta Systems

Cline,T. (1998) Learning to read for meaning. National Association for Language Development in the Curriculum (NALDIC) Conference paper. Unpublished.

Collier, V.P. (1987) Age and rate of acquisition of second language for academic purposes. *TESOL Quarterly*, 21, 617-641

Collier, V.P. (1992) A synthesis of studies examining long-term language minority student data on academic achievement. *Bilingual Research Journal*, 16(1-2), 187-212

Collier, V.P. (1999) How long? A synthesis of research on academic achievement in a second language. *TESOL Quarterly*, 23, 509-531

Collier, V.P. and Thomas, W.P. (1989) How quickly can immigrants become proficient in school English? *Journal of Educational Issues of Language Minority Students.* 5, 26-38

Collier, V.P. and Thomas, W. P. School Effectiveness for Language Minority Students. In collected papers of the *Invitational Conference on Teaching and Learning English as an Additional Language*, London, 27-28 April 1995. London: SCAA

Commission for Racial Equality (1986) *The Calderdale Report.* London: CRE

Corson, D. (1997) The learning and use of academic English words. *Language Learning*, 47, 671-718

Crawford, J. (1997) Best evidence: Research foundations of the Bilingual Education Act. Washington, DC: National Clearinghouse for Bilingual Education [www.ncbe.gwu.edu]

Cummins, J. (1981a) The role of primary language development in promoting educational success for language minority students. In California State Department of Education (Ed.), *Schooling and language minority students: A theoretical framework.* Evaluation, Dissemination and Assessment Center, California State University, Los Angeles

Cummins, J. (1981b) Age on arrival and immigrant second language learning in Canada. A reassessment. *Applied Linguistics*, 2, 132-149

Cummins, J. (1991a) The development of bilingual proficiency from home to school: A longitudinal study of Portuguese-speaking children. *Journal of Education*, 173, 85-98

Cummins, J. (1991b) Interdependence of first- and second-language proficiency in bilingual children. In E. Bialystok (Ed.) *Language processing in bilingual children* (pp. 70-89). Cambridge: Cambridge University Press

Cummins, J. (1992) Language Proficiency, Bilingualism, and Academic Achievement. In Richard-Amato, P.A. and Snow, M.A. (eds) *The Multilingual Classroom*. New York: Longman

Cummins, J. (1996) *Negotiating identities: Education for empowerment in a diverse society*. Los Angeles: California Association for Bilingual Education

Cummins, J. and Corson, D. (Eds.). (1998) *Bilingual education*. Dordrecht, The Netherlands: Kluwer Academic Publishers

Cummins, J., Harley, B., Swain, M., and Allen, P. (1990) Social and individual factors in the development of bilingual proficiency. In B. Harley, P. Allen, J. Cummins, and M. Swain (Eds.) *The development of second language proficiency*. (pp. 119-133). Cambridge: Cambridge University Press

Cummins, J., Swain, M., Nakajima, K., Handscombe, J., Green, D. and Tran, C. (1984) Linguistic interdependence among Japanese immigrant students. In C. Rivera (Ed.) *Communicative competence approaches to language proficiency assessment: Research and application*. (pp. 60-81). Clevedon, Avon: Multilingual Matters

Curriculum Corporation (1994) *ESL scales*. Carlton, Victoria, Curriculum Corporation

Davies, A. (1991) *The Native Speaker in Applied Linguistics*: Edinburgh University Press

Davies, A., Grove, E. and Wilkes, M. (1997) Review of literature on acquiring literacy in a second language. In P.McKay, A. Davies, B. Devlin, J. Clayton, R. Oliver and S. Zammit (Principal Researchers) *The bilingual interface project report* (pp.17-74). Canberra, Australia, Department of Employment, Education, Training and Youth Affairs

Davison, C. (1995) Learning language, learning content: trends in ESL curriculum planning and assessment in Australia. In *Invitational Conference on Teaching and Learning English as Additional Language* (pp.70-99). London, School Curriculum and Assessment Authority

Department for Education and Employment (1995) *Key Stages 1 and 2 of the National Curriculum*: HMSO

Department for Education and Employment (1998) *The National Literacy Strategy: framework for teaching*. London DfEE

Delpit, L. (1988) The silenced dialogue: Power and pedagogy in educating other people's children. *Harvard Educational Review*, 58, 280-298

Delpit, L. (1997, Fall). Ebonics and culturally responsive instruction. *Rethinking Schools*, 12:1, 6-7

Dörnyei, Z. (1998) Motivation in second and foreign language learning. *Language Teaching*, 31, pp.117-135

Edelsky, C. (1991) *With literacy and justice for all: Rethinking the social in language and education*. London Falmer Press

Edwards, V. and Redfern, A. (1992) *The world in a classroom*. Clevedon, Multilingual Matters

Edwards, V. and Walker, S. (in press) Language and design in multilingual classrooms. In M. Martin-Jones and M. Saxena (eds) *Bilingual support in the mainstream classroom.* Clevedon: Multilingual Matters.

Edwards, V. (1998) *The power of Babel: teaching and learning in multilingual classrooms.* Stoke on Trent: Trentham Books.

Elley, W.B. (1991). Acquiring literacy in a second language: The effect of book-based programs. *Language Learning,* 41, 375-411

Elley, W.B. and Manghubai, F. (1983) The impact of reading on second language learning. *Reading Research Quarterly,* 19, 53-67

Ellis, R. (1994) *The study of second language acquisition.* Oxford, Oxford University Press

Fielding, L.G. and Pearson, P.D. (1994) Reading comprehension: what works. *Educational Leadership,* 51(5), 62-68

First Steps (undated) *Supporting linguistic and cultural diversity through First Steps: the Highgate Project..* http://www.heinemann.com/firststeps/res11/html

Fitzgerald, J. (1995a) English-as-a-second-language learners' cognitive reading processes: A review of research in the United States. *Review of Educational Research,* 65, 145-190

Fitzgerald, J. (1995b) English-as-a-second-language reading instruction in the United States: A research review. *Journal of Reading Behavior,* 27, 115-152

Frangoudaki, A. and Dragonas, T. (1997) 'What is our Homeland?' *Ethnocentrism and Education,* Athens, Alexandria

Frederickson, N.L. and Frith, U. (1998) Identifying dyslexia in bilingual children: A phonological approach with Inner London Sylheti speakers. *Dyslexia* 4, p.119

Foster, P. (1998) A classroom perspective on the negiotiation of meaning. *Applied Linguistics,* 19(1), pp1-23

Foster, S. (1990) *The Communicative Competence of Young Children*: Longman

Gabina, J.J. *et al.* (1986) *EIFE. Influence of factors on the learning of Basque.* Gasteiz: Central Publications Service of the Basque Country

Genesee, F. (Ed.) (1999) *Program alternatives for linguisitically diverse students* (Educational Practice Report No. 1). Washington, DC: Center for Applied Linguistics and Center for Research on Education, Diversity and Excellence [www.crede.ucsc.edu]

Genesee, F. (1979) Acquisition of reading skills in immersion programs. *Foreign Language Annals,* 12, 71-77

Gibbon, P. and Scott, S. (eds) (1998) *Sharing Practice in Intercultural Education* (series). Intercultural Education Partnership UK

Gibbons, P. (1991) *Learning to Learn in a Second Language.* Australia: Primary English Teaching Association

Gillborn, D. and Gipps, C. (1996) *Recent research on the achievements of ethnic minority pupils.* London, HMSO

Gillham, B. (ed) (1986) *The Language of School Subjects*. London: Heinemann Educational Books

Gonczi, A. (1994) Competency based assessments in the professions in Australia. *Assessment in Education*, 1(1), pp. 27-44

Gregory, E. (ed) (1997) *One Child, Many Worlds: Early Learning in Multicultural Communities*. London: David Fulton

Gregory, E. and Williams, A. (1998) 'Home and school literacy practices in two East London communities': paper presented at the 31st Annual Conference of the British Association of Applied Linguistics

Hakuta, K. (1986) *Mirror of language*. New York: Basic Books

Halliday, M. A. K. (1975) *Learning How to Mean*: London: Arnold

Hamers, J. F. and Blanc, M. (1982) 'Towards a social-psychological model of bilingual development', *Journal of Language and Social Psychology* 1: 29 49

Harris, R. (1997) Romantic Bilingualism: Time for a Change? in English as an Additional Language: Changing Perspectives, National Association for Language Developement In the Curriculum (NALDIC)

Hornberger, N. (1995) Creating Successful Learning Contexts for Bilingual Literacy in Garcia, O. and Baker, C (eds) *Policy and Practice in Bilingual Education: Extending the Foundations*. Clevedon, Avon: Multilingual Matters

Jones, L. and Moore, R. (1995) Appropriating competence: the competency movement, the New Right and the 'culture change' project. *British Journal of Education and Work*, 8(2), pp.78-92

Jordan, R. and Powell, S. (1995) *Understanding and Teaching Children with Autism*: London: Wiley

Kamiol, R. (1990) Second language acquisition through immersion in daycare. *Journal of Child Language* 17: 147-70

Klesmer, H. (1994) Assessment and teacher perceptions of ESL student achievement. *English Quarterly*, 26(3), 5-7

Krashen, S. (1982) *Principles and Practice in Second Language Acquisition*: London; Pergamon Press

Krashen, S. (1993) *The power of reading*. Englewood, CO: Libraries Unlimited

Kuhn, T.S. (1962/70) *The structure of scientific revolutions*. Chicago, University of Chicago Press

Lee, J-W. and Schallert, D.L. (1997) The relative contribution of L2 language proficiency and L1 reading ability to L2 reading performance: A test of the threshold hypothesis in an EFL context. *TESOL Quarterly*, 31, 713-739

Lightbown, P.M. (1992) Can they do it themselves? A comprehension-based ESL course for young children. In R. Courchene, J.J. Glidden, J. St. John, and C. Therien (Eds.) *Comprehension-based second language teaching*. Ottawa: University of Ottawa Press

Lindholm, K.J. (1990) Bilingual immersion education: Criteria for program development. In A.M. Padilla, H.H. Fairchild and C.M. Valadez (Eds.), *Bilingual education: Issues and strategies* (pp.91-105). London: SAGE

Lindholm, K.J. and Aclan, Z. (1991) Bilingual Proficiency as a bridge to academic achievement: Results from bilingual/immersion programs. *Journal of Education*, 173, 99-113

Lo Bianco, J. (1998) ESL... is it migrant lunacy? ... is it history? *Australian Language Matters*, Apr/May/June, 1-6-7

Malherbe, E.G. (1946) *The bilingual school*. Johannesberg: The Bilingual School Association

McKay, P. (1998) The literacy benchmarks and ESL. *Australian Council of TESOL Associations Background Paper No.2 Literacy ESL broadbanding benchmarking*. Melbourne

McKay, P. (co-ordinator) (1992) *ESL development: language and literacy in schools project, vol.1*. East Melbourne, Victoria, National Languages and Literacy Institute of Australia

McNamara, T. (1996) *Measuring second language performance*. London, Longman

Meek, M. (1988) *How texts teach what readers learn*. Stroud: The Thimble Press

National Association for Language Development in the Curriculum (1998) *Provision in literacy hours for pupils learning English as an Additional Language*: NALDIC

National Curriculum Council (1991) *Circular number 11: linguistic diversity and the National Curriculum*. York: NCC

National Research Council. (1998) *Preventing reading difficulties in young children*. Washington, DC: National Academy Press

Nagy, W.E., Garcia, G.E., Durgunoglu, A., and Hancin-Bhatt, B. (1993) Spanish-English bilingual students' use of cognates in English reading. *Journal of Reading Behaviour*, 25, 241-259

Nagy, W.E., Herman, P.A., and Anderson, R.C. (1985) Learning words from context. *Reading Research Quarterly*, 20(2): 233-253

Nation, P. and Coady, J. (1988) Vocabulary and reading. In R. Carter and M. McCarthy (Eds.) *Vocabulary and language teaching*. (97-110) London: Longman

Office for Standards in Education (1997) *The assessment of the language development of bilingual pupils*. London, OFSTED

Office for Standards in Education (1998) *Inspecting Subjects 3-11 Guidance for Inspectors*. London, OFSTED

Office for Standards in Education (1999) *Inspecting Subjects and Aspects 11-18 English as an Additional Language*. London, OFSTED

Office for Standards in Education (1999a) *Setting in Primary Schools*. London, OFSTED

Ogbu, J. (1978) *Minority education and caste*. New York: Academic Press

Ovando, C.J. and Collier, V.P. (1998) *Bilingual and ESL classrooms: Teaching in multicultural contexts* (2nd ed.). Boston: McGraw-HIll

Pena-Hughes, E. and Solis, J. (1980) ABCs (unpublished report). McAllen, TX: McAllen Independent School District

Perera, K. (1984) *Children's writing and reading: analysing classroom language.* Oxford: Basil Blackwell

Postlethwaite, T.N. and Ross, K.N. (1992) *Effective schools in reading: Implications for educational planners An exploratory study.* The Hague: The International Association for the Evaluation of Educational Achievement

Ramirez, J.D. (1992) Executive summary. *Bilingual Research Journal,* 16, 1-62

Rampton, B. (1990) 'Displacing the 'native speaker': expertise, affiliation and inheritance', *English Language Teaching Journal,* vol 44 no 2: 87-101

Rea-Dickinson, P. and Gardner, S. (1998) 'The roles of literacy and oracy assessment in bilingual intervention projects': paper presented at the 31st Annual Conference of the British Association of Applied Linguistics

Reid, E. (1988) 'Linguistic minorities and language education – the English experience', *Journal of Multilingual and Multicultural Development* 9, 1 and 2: 181-191

Reyes, M. de la Luz. (1994) Challenging venerable assumptions: Literacy instruction for linguistically different students. *Harvard Educational Review,* 62, 427-446

Rossell, C.H. and Baker, K. (1996) The effectiveness of bilingual education. *Research in the Teaching of English,* 30, 7-74

Sahgal, A. and Agnihotri, R. K. (1985) 'Syntax – the common bond. Acceptability of syntactic deviances in Indian English', *English Worldwide* 6, 1: 117-129

SCAA (1996) *Teaching English as an additional language: a framework for policy.* London, School Curriculum and Assessment Authority

Schmidt, R.W. (1990) The role of consciousness in second language learning. *Applied Linguistics,* 11(2), pp.129-158

Sierra, J. and Olaziregi, I. (1989) *EIFE 2. Influence of factors on the learning of Basque.* Gasteiz: Central Publications Service of the Basque Country

Sierra, J. and Olaziregi, I. (1991) *EIFE 3. Influence of factors on the learning of Basque. Study of the models A, B and D in second year Basic General Education.* Gasteiz: Central Publications Service of the Basque Country

Skehan, P. (1998) *A cognitive approach to language learning.* Oxford, oxford University Press

Spolsky, B. (1989) *Conditions for second language learning.* Oxford, Oxford University Press

Swain, M. (1995) Three functions of output in second language learning. In G. Cook and B.Seidlhofer (eds), *Principle and practice in applied linguistics* (pp.125-144). Oxford, Oxford University Press

Swann (1985) *Education for All,* Department of Education and Science

TESOL (1997) EAL standards for Pre-K-12 students. Alexandria, VA: TESOL Inc

Thomas, W.P. and Collier, V.P. (1997a) *School effectiveness for language minority students.* Washington, DC: National Clearinghouse for Bilingual Education [www.ncbe.gwu.edu}

Thomas, W.P. and Collier, V.P. (1997b) Two languages are better than one. *Educational Leadership*, 55 (4), 23-26

Thomas, W.P. and Collier, V.P. (1999a) Accelerated schooling for English language learners. *Educational Leadership*, 56 (17), 46-49

Thomas, W.P. and Collier, V.P. (1999b) *A national study of school effectiveness for language minority students' long-term academic achievement. Overview of research design.* Santa Cruz, CA: Center for Research on Education, Diversity and Excellence [www.crede.ucsc.edu]

Tizard, J., Schofield, W.N. and Hewison, J. (1982) Collaboration between teachers and parents in assisting children's reading. *British Journal of Educational Psychology*, 52, 1-15

Tosi, A. (1996) *Learning from diversity: language education and intercultural relations in the inner city.* Brussels, European Commission and Eurocities

Townsend, H.E.R. (1970) *Immigrant Pupils in England*: NFER

Travers, P. (ed.) (1999) *Enabling progress in a multilingual classroom: towards inclusive education.* London Borough of Enfield, Language and Curriculum Access Service

Truscott, J. (1998) Noticing in second language acquisition: a critical review. *Second Language Research*, 14(2), pp.103-135

Valdés, G. (1997) Dual-language immersion programs: a cautionary note concerning the education of language-minority students. *Harvard Educational Review*, 67(3), pp.391-429

Verhoeven, L. (1991) Acquisition of biliteracy. In J.H. Hulstijn and J.F. Matter (Eds.) *Reading in two languages.* Amsterdam: AILA. AILA Review, 8, 61-74

Verhoeven, L. (1994) Transfer in bilingual development: the linguistic interdependence hypothesis revisited. *Language Learning*, 44, 381-415

Wells, G. (1986) *The meaning makers.* Portsmouth, NH:Heinemann

Widdowson, H. (1993) 'The ownership of English', 1993 Conference Report of the International Association of Teaching English as a Foreign Language

Wong Fillmore, L. (1997) *Authentic literature in ESL instruction.* Glenview, IL: ScottForesman

Wong Fillmore, L. (1991) Second language learning in children: A model of language learning in social context. In E. Bialystok (Ed.) *Language processing in bilingual children* (pp.49-69). Cambridge: Cambridge University Press